A NATURAL HISTORY
OF MARINE MAMMALS

Figure 1   Harbor seal

A Natural History of Marine Mammals

Victor B. Scheffer

Illustrations by Peter Parnall

Charles Scribner's Sons ⌇ New York

Copyright © 1976 Victor B. Scheffer

Library of Congress Cataloging in Publication Data

Scheffer, Victor B
    A natural history of marine mammals.

    Bibliography: p. 145
    Includes index.
    1. Marine mammals. I. Parnall, Peter. II. Title.
QL713.2.S33   599′.09′2   76-14820
ISBN 0-684-14576-6

Portion of "quote and only man is vile quote," copyright 1933 by Doubleday & Company, Inc. from the book *the lives and times of archy and mehitabel* by Don Marquis. Reprinted by permission of Doubleday & Company, Inc., and Faber & Faber Ltd.

The illustration on page 4 was redesigned, with permission, from a drawing by S. J. Proctor and Greg Davies, published in the booklet *Whales: Their Story*, by the Vancouver Aquarium.

1 3 5 7 9 11 13 15 17 19 v/c 20 18 16 14 12 10 8 6 4 2

Printed in the United States of America

Contents

PREFACE

Within the animal kingdom are 111 species of unusual beasts known as the marine mammals. They are warm-blooded, they nurse their young with milk, and, with few exceptions, they gain their living from the sea. (The exceptions are a few species which live in fresh water.) The marine mammals vary in shape and size from the young sea otter, which at first glance could be taken for a puppy dog, to the great blue whale, a superbeast whose glistening body reaches a length of 100 feet and a weight of 200 tons.

This book tells how the marine mammals evolved from land ancestors and how they met and overcame the challenges of a cold, wet, vast, and salty ocean. It describes the peculiar features of anatomy, physiology, and behavior which characterize the various species.

Marine mammals challenge the scientist to explore their accommodations to life—that is, to find out how they are able to feed and breed in the sea. Some of the answers from research have practical value, others simply add to the richness of our lives, by enlarging our awareness.

Scientists are drawn to study the marine mammals because these creatures represent extremes in the animal kingdom. For the same reason, scientists are interested in shrews, the smallest of land mammals; elephants, the largest; bats, which have conquered the air; and moles, which blindly tunnel the earth and devour daily one-half of their own body weight.

People other than scientists have found the marine mammals of interest for bread-and-butter reasons. The large bodies of many species are rich in oil and protein; some are covered with valuable fur. Marine mammals provide a living for coastal Indians, Aleuts, and Eskimos. They also provide goods for world markets; their products of commerce number in the thousands. In this book, however, I am not concerned with the commercial uses of the beasts of the sea but with the ways they move, and live, and have their being.

Little is yet known about some of the rare and remote kinds of marine mammals. No one has yet seen a newborn Ross seal; no one knows the color of its coat. The Tasman beaked whale and the pygmy right whale are known only from stranded specimens; nothing is known of their lives. I have tried to call attention to what is unknown, as well as what is known, about marine mammals, for there is attraction in the mystery as well as the certainty of their lives.

Three new windows into the lives of the marine mammals are opening to an interested public today—

the animal television show, the oceanarium (or large saltwater aquarium), and the wildlife expedition (or camera safari). Millions of people are now learning about kinds of animals which a few years ago were known only to specialists.

The more we learn about them, the more we realize that each is marvelously successful in its own animal way. Though this one or that one may seem to imitate human behavior, it is acting on different impulses. Almost everything it does, it does from instincts which were programmed into its body at the moment of conception. Though it may be self-taught by experience, it is never educated.

Don Marquis's archy, the poetic cockroach, in a flash of insight, made a comment which is appropriate here:

> as a representative of the insect world
> i have often wondered
> on what man bases his claims
> to superiority
> everything he knows he has had
> to learn whereas we insects are born
> knowing everything we need to know

A NATURAL HISTORY
OF MARINE MAMMALS

1. THE FOSSIL RECORD

Six Lines of Descent

The living marine mammals are descended from six zoological groups, each representing a line of ancestors which, long ago and independently of other lines, deserted the land to live in the sea. The six groups are listed here, each under a common or vernacular name. Their origins are outlined in the table on pages 10–11, and their places in the formal zoological scheme are shown in Appendix II.

Sea otters, 1 species only.

Walking seals, 15 species, including the fur seals, sea lions, and walruses. All can walk on four legs. Because they have visible ears, they are often called "eared" seals.

Crawling seals, 17 species, including the harbor seal, gray seal, elephant seal, monk seal, and polar seals. The hind legs of these seals cannot support their bodies. Crawling seals hump along like great caterpillars. Because they have inconspicuous ears which are little more than skin membranes flush

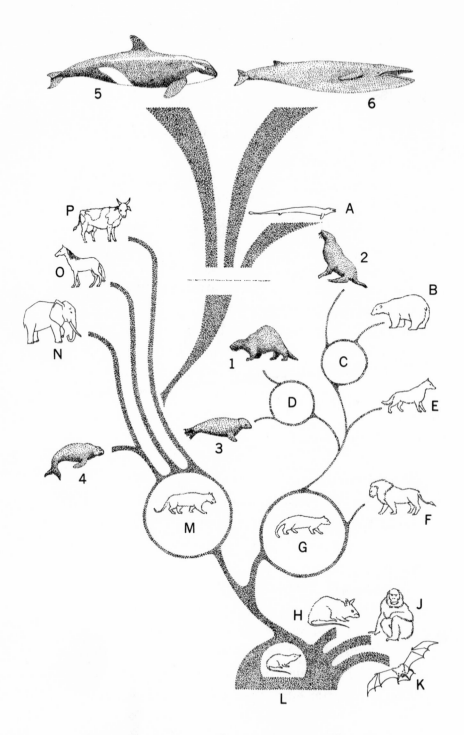

Figure 2 Origins of the marine mammal groups
(see key, opposite)

with the sides of the head, they are often called "earless" seals. Collectively, the walking and crawling seals are known as the pinnipeds (literally, those with "winged feet").

Sirenians, 4 species, including the manatees and dugongs, all tropical.

Toothed cetaceans, 64 species. The larger ones, such as the sperm whale, are called whales. The smaller ones are called dolphins or porpoises or are given special names such as beluga and narwhal. Throughout this book the name porpoise is used for all the small cetaceans.

Baleen cetaceans, 10 species. All are called whales and all have baleen plates in the upper jaw instead of teeth. These curious plates, used in feeding, are described in Chapter 4.

ORIGINS OF THE MARINE MAMMAL GROUPS
KEY TO DIAGRAM/FIGURE 2

The Groups

1	Sea otters	4	Sirenians
2	Walking seals	5	Toothed cetaceans
3	Crawling seals	6	Baleen cetaceans

Their Relatives (*ancient forms in italic type*)

A	*Archaeocetes*	J	Primates
B	Bears	K	Bats
C	*Stem bears*	L	*Stem insectivores*
D	*Stem otters*	M	*Stem ungulates*
E	Dogs	N	Elephants
F	Cats	O	Horses
G	*Stem carnivores*	P	Cattle
H	Rodents		

From the Land to the Sea

Life began in the ocean at least 3 billion years ago. It started in particles which were little more than chemical bits having the power to grow and to divide. Life stayed in the ocean for about two and a half billion years. Then the first land plants appeared, followed by land animals of greater and greater complexity. Rather soon in the geologic time scale, reptiles, birds, and mammals evolved and diversified into tens of thousands of species. Some moved to one or more of all of the continents.

Meanwhile, in the ocean, great reptiles had begun to flourish. They were beautifully accommodated to marine life. One known as a plesiosaur was 50 feet long. All disappeared without a trace about 100 million years ago when the world climate turned cold.

Later a few of the land reptiles, birds, and mammals returned to the sea, their ancestral home. These repatriates were the forebears of modern sea turtles and sea snakes, sea birds such as penguins and albatrosses, and the marine mammals. The modern marine mammals did not evolve directly, in the ocean, from any of the marine reptiles. Rather, they spent millions of years on land developing "warm-bloodedness" before they turned back to the mother sea.

Not only does the evidence of fossils show that the ancestors of the marine mammals were land creatures; this is proved also by vestigial organs in living species. These organs are relics of the past. Before the baleen

Figure 3 Desmostylus (*restored*)

whale is born it has a set of tiny teeth—completely useless and doomed never to harden or break through the gum. Most cetaceans have a few bristly hairs at birth, while some species keep them throughout life. Porpoises have hind-leg buds for a few weeks during fetal life. As adults, they have vestigial "hips," which are no more than a pair of slender bones floating in the muscles near the sex organs. Very rarely, a whale or a porpoise—perhaps one in a hundred thousand—is actually born with useless, partly formed legs.

A few marine mammals of ancient times were failures; their bloodlines are extinct. Bones of *Desmostylus,* a large marine mammal shaped like a hippopotamus, are rather common in rocky beds 10 million to 30 million years old. To judge from its skeleton and teeth, the beast waded in shallow bays and fed on shellfish.

Some kinds of land mammals could be called nearly marine; they live at the edge of the sea and feed upon saltwater fish or shellfish. Most of them, like the raccoon, land otter, mink, weasel, and Arctic fox, are merely opportunists. They will hunt on beaches or in tidal waters but will get along equally well inland. Others, like the polar bear, the Cape Horn otters, and the fishing bats of Tiburon Island, Mexico, are more dependent upon marine food, yet these too can only be called dabblers in the sea. It is clear that within the mammalian class a natural experiment is still under way, in which some species are moving from the land toward the sea.

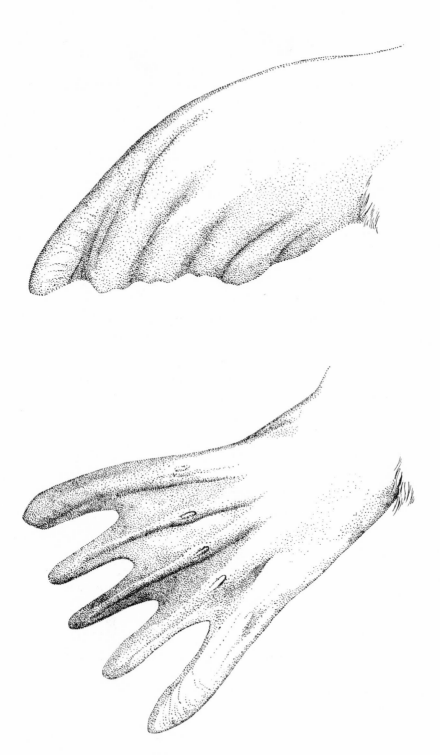

Figure 4   Sea lion flippers

A Natural History of Marine Mammals

The results of that experiment—that drift toward aquatic life—are plainly seen within the subdivisions of marine mammals as well as within the mammalian class as a whole. The shapes of marine mammal feet are a simple clue to the time distance (long or short) which separates each of the six groups from its ancestral home on land. That is, one can arrange the six groups in the order of their newness to the sea.

The sea otter has kept rather ordinary front paws,

Origins of Marine Mammal Groups

		Land ancestor
Group	Supposed age (millions of years)	Original Stock
sea otter	5	crab-eating land otter
walking seals	30	bearlike carnivore
crawling seals	30	otterlike carnivore
sirenians	55	primitive hoofed mammal
toothed cetaceans	60	primitive hoofed mammal
baleen cetaceans	60	primitive hoofed mammal

* All fossils are those of extinct genera except those of *Enhydra,* which is the genus of the modern sea otter.

** The archaeocetes, slightly more primitive cetaceans, are repre-

though its hind feet have become flippers. (A flipper is a hand or foot, flattened and often webbed, adapted for use as a paddle or steering vane.) Within the walking seal and crawling seal groups, both the hands and the feet have become flippers. The sirenians have lost their hind legs entirely but have kept the flexible use of their front flippers for swimming and for walking under water among sea grasses. The toothed and baleen cetaceans have also lost their hind legs, while their arms have become rigid from the shoulder out.

Earliest known fossil *

Known age (millions of years)	Genus	Where found
2	*Enhydra*	Pacific North America
20	*Enaliarctos*	California
20	genus(?) fragment of leg bone	Europe
45	*Protosiren;* others	Europe; Africa
40	*Agorophius;* others **	North America; England; Egypt
30	*Pachycetus*	Europe

sented in fossil deposits 45 million years old. These animals cannot be definitely related to the lines of modern cetaceans, either toothed or baleen; they disappeared 25 million years ago.

11

2. MARINE MAMMALS TODAY

The six groups of marine mammals can be thought of as six separate launching parties from the continents to the oceans. Each is a distinct evolutionary group. In formal zoological classification, however, the six groups cover a total of fourteen families. Each family contains one or more genera, and each genus contains one or more species. (See Appendix II.)

A typical present-day species from each of the families has been selected for description in terms of body weight, geographic range, and population numbers. Gaps indicate that the animal's life history is still imperfectly known.

Sea otter

Sea otter group (only species), family Mustelidae, species *Enhydra lutris*. Body weight of males reaches 100 pounds, of females 72 pounds; a newborn pup averages 4.5 pounds. Sea otters are found only along the shores of the North Pacific Ocean. Their population is about 120,000 in the United States and 10,000 in the Soviet Union.

Figure 5   Sea otter

Steller sea lion

Walking seal group, family Otariidae, species *Eumetopias jubatus*. Named after Georg Wilhelm Steller, the German naturalist who first studied the animal in 1741–1742. Body weight of males reaches 2,240 pounds, of females 605 pounds; a newborn pup averages 40 pounds. Steller sea lions live only along the shores of the North Pacific Ocean. Their population is about 225,000 in the United States and 25,000 in the Soviet Union.

Pacific walrus

Walking seal group, family Odobenidae, species *Odobenus rosmarus*. Body weight of males reaches 3,433 pounds, of females 2,342 pounds; a newborn pup averages 150 pounds. Pacific walruses remain the year around in the Bering and Chukchi seas and in the Arctic Ocean between Alaska and Siberia. Their world population is 180,00 to 200,000.

Harbor seal

Crawling seal group, family Phocidae, species *Phoca vitulina*. Body weight of males reaches 256 pounds, of females 243 pounds; a newborn pup averages 28 pounds. Harbor seals are widely distributed in the temperate and cool waters of North America, Asia, and Europe. Their world population is perhaps 600,000.

Figure 6   Steller sea lion

Figure 7   Pacific walrus

Figure 8 Harbor seal

Dugong

Sirenian group, family Dugongidae, species *Dugong dugon*. Little is known about the body weight, which perhaps reaches 800 pounds. There is only one species; it lives in tropical bays of the Indian and western Pacific oceans. In United States waters it is found only at Palau. Though groups numbering hundreds are seen off Somalia and northern Australia, the world population is believed to be only a few thousands.

Caribbean manatee

Sirenian group, family Trichechidae, species *Trichechus manatus*. The family contains three species which closely resemble one another. Body weight of the Caribbean manatee reaches 1,300 pounds; a newborn calf weighs 40 to 60 pounds. This species lives in coastal streams and saltwater bays of the warm Caribbean region, including Florida, eastern Central America, and northern South America. To "census" this shy and secretive animal is almost impossible. There are thought to be about 1,000 in Florida.

Chinese lake porpoise

Toothed cetacean group, family Platanistidae, species *Lipotes vexillifer*. Adults reach a body weight of 240 pounds. Found only in Tung Ting Lake, China, and in lower reaches of the streams that flow into the lake. In the dry season, these porpoises herd together in shallow pools. Their population is only a few hundreds.

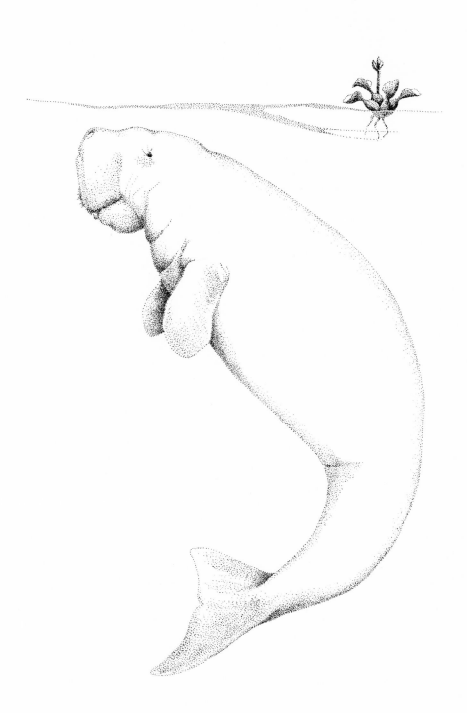

Figure 9   Dugong

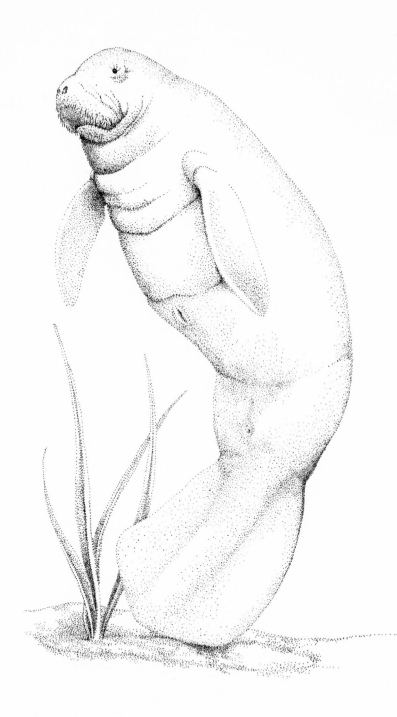

Figure 10   Caribbean manatee

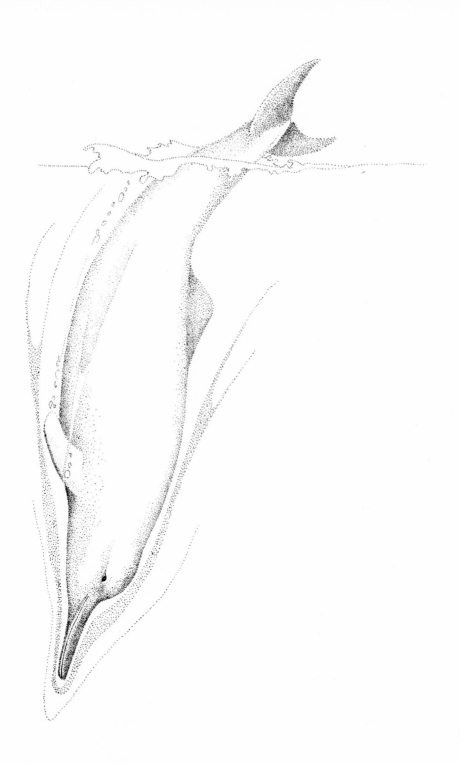

Figure 11   Chinese lake porpoise

Figure 12   Bottlenose porpoise

Bottlenose porpoise

Toothed cetacean group, family Delphinidae, species *Tursiops truncatus*. Adults reach a body weight of 850 pounds; a newborn calf weighs about 30 pounds. The bottlenose porpoise is easily tamed and is the cetacean most often seen in oceanariums. In the wild it lives in temperate and tropical waters of the world, usually near shore where its food—small schooling fish—is plentiful. In the whole world there may be hundreds of thousands of bottlenose porpoises.

Beluga

Toothed cetacean group, family Monodontidae, species *Delphinapterus leucas.* Also called white whale. Body weight in males reaches 3,500 pounds; females are slightly smaller; a newborn calf averages 173 pounds. Belugas live only in the Arctic Ocean and nearby seas. They may travel in search of food for a distance of several hundred miles up large rivers. Their total population is perhaps tens of thousands.

Sperm whale

Toothed cetacean group, family Physeteridae, species *Physeter catodon.* By far the largest of the toothed cetacean group, the adult males reach a weight of 60 tons, the females 16 tons. The newborn calf averages about 1 ton. Moby Dick, in Herman Melville's novel of that name, was a sperm whale. His kind live in all seas except those near polar ice. Their world population is about 640,000, or 70 percent of its size before the era of modern whaling.

Baird beaked whale

Toothed cetacean group, family Ziphiidae, species *Berardius bairdi.* Also known as giant bottlenose whale. Adults reach a weight of about 12 tons, which makes them barely attractive to commercial whalers. The female is slightly larger than the male; a newborn calf weighs about 1 ton. Though beaked whales are widely distributed in the world ocean, this one lives only in the North Pacific Ocean and adjacent seas. Its population is perhaps thousands.

Figure 13   Beluga

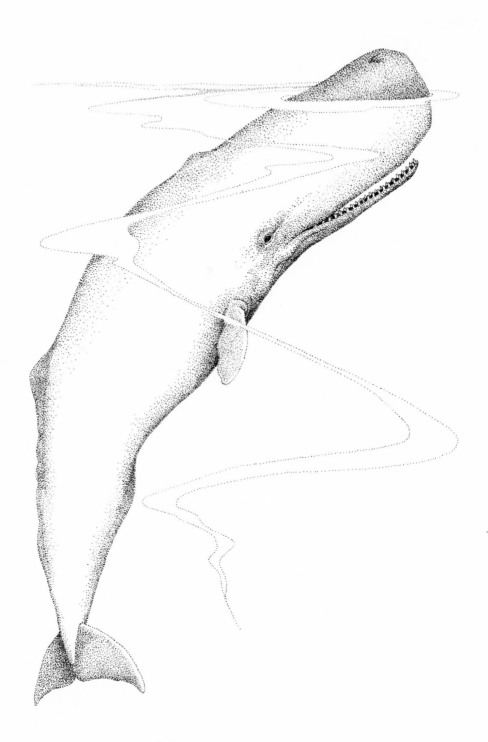

Figure 14 Sperm whale

Figure 15   Baird beaked whale

Marine Mammals Today

Gray whale

Baleen cetacean group, family Eschrichtiidae, species *Eschrichtius robustus*. Named after D. F. Eschricht, a European anatomist who studied whales a century ago. Body weight of the male reaches 25 tons; of the pregnant female 40 tons; of the newborn calf about 900 pounds. This remarkable whale is in a family by itself. It breeds in shallow marine waters of Baja California, Mexico, and migrates into the Bering, Chukchi, and Okhotsk seas. The population is about 11,000 and is threatened by industrial and tourist invasions of its breeding waters.

Humpback whale

Baleen cetacean group, family Balaenopteridae, species *Megaptera novaeangliae*. Body weight of adults reaches 45 tons; of the newborn calf slightly under 1 ton. Humpbacks live in all oceans, most of them wintering in tropical waters and summering in temperate or cool waters. Their world population has been reduced by over-hunting from about 50,000 to about 7,000, or 14 percent of the original numbers.

Bowhead whale

Baleen cetacean group, family Balaenidae, species *Balaena mysticetus*. Also known as Greenland right whale. Body weight of adults reaches 110 tons (mostly fat); of the newborn calf about 2½ tons. Bowheads are confined to the Arctic Ocean and nearby seas. Since about 1915 they have been hunted by

Figure 16   Gray whale

Figure 17   Humpback whale

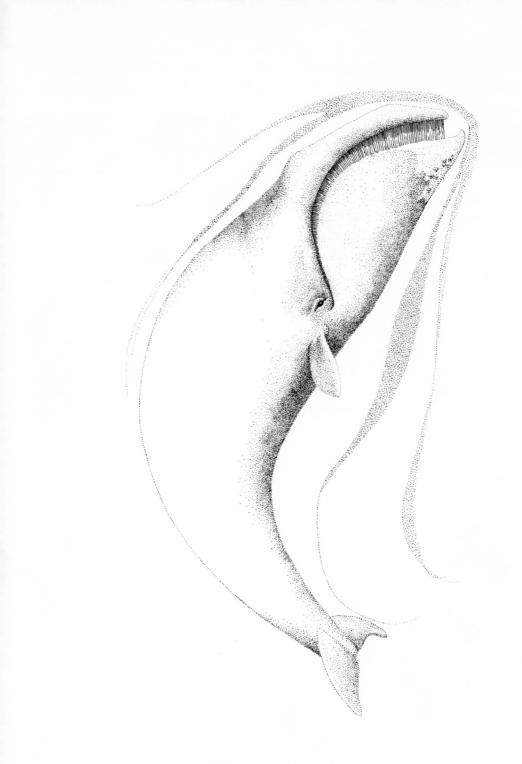

Figure 18   Bowhead whale

natives only. They may have numbered more than 10,000 before commercial whaling began in the nineteenth century; today perhaps 2,000. They are difficult to count because they live for months at a time in ice-strewn waters which are unfriendly to ships and small aircraft.

3. CHALLENGES OF OCEAN LIFE

More than 99 percent of the globe's animated envelope is oceanic. Though the ocean may seem to be a watery desert, it is in fact a pasture which contributes one-third of the organic production of the world. The living organisms of the sea were responsible for attracting the first marine mammals away from the land. Here in the ocean they found fish and squid, shellfish, sea grasses, and other new foods.

But they had to pay a price. They were now in a habitat which was cold, fluid, three-dimensional, and salty. How did they meet these challenges? What evolutionary changes in body shape took place while they were filling their ecological niches in the sea?

The Challenge of Cold

As compared with most land habitats, the ocean is cool. The thermal conductivity of water is about twenty times that of air. A naked man, though comfortable in 90-degree air, will soon chill in 90-degree water. Seals of the polar regions live in water which is less than one degree above freezing, while during the long winter they never see the sun. Even the monk seals and the dugongs, though they live in warm climates, must somehow maintain their body heat.

All marine mammals are large-bodied. To withstand the cold, the smallest pelagic (open sea) species must weigh at least 10 to 15 pounds. This is the weight to which some Alaskan fur seal pups drop during their first harsh winter at sea. Though a sea otter pup is even smaller—starting life at 4 to 5 pounds—it spends many hours each day snuggled against its mother's fur. The physical principle involved here is that, if a smaller and a larger object of similar shape and material are placed in ice water, the smaller one chills more quickly. It is fortunate that marine mammals, supported as they are by the buoyancy of water, can "afford" to have larger bodies than can land mammals.

At birth, marine mammals are precocious (early developed). Unlike kittens and puppies, marine mammals are wide-eyed and active at the time when they draw their first breath. A newborn fur seal already has a third of its permanent teeth in place! A fur seal mother weighing 100 pounds will give birth to a 15-pound pup. (This would be comparable to a 133-pound woman's giving birth to a 20-pound baby.) All marine mammals *can* swim at birth, though only the sirenians and cetaceans *must* do so.

A Natural History of Marine Mammals

Marine mammals are insulated by jackets of fur, or blubber, or both. Blubber is the thick layer resembling bacon fat which lies just under the skin.

The rich, velvety coat of the fur seal has 300,000 hairs per square inch; that of the sea otter, 600,000 hairs. On healthy animals, the fur never gets wet down to the skin. Millions of tiny air bubbles remain trapped in the oily underfur and provide thermal insulation. A sea otter must spend nearly half of its waking hours in cleaning and fluffing its fur.

All marine mammals except the sea otter have the blubber layer. It is richly supplied with blood vessels and, in whales, is up to 2 feet thick. When workmen, using power tackle, remove the blubber of a whale, it comes off like the peel of an orange. The blubber of a big walrus or elephant seal amounts to one-third of the body weight, while the blubber of a ringed seal in winter can reach nearly one-half of the body weight. This is a good thing, for ringed seals resting on ice are exposed to winds as low as 40 degrees below zero.

Marine mammals have a special kind of blood-vessel system which provides counter-current heat exchange. That is, the arteries which carry warm blood to the flippers, tail, and other extremities are closely surrounded by veins which carry colder blood back to the deep body. Some of the arterial heat which might otherwise be lost to the sea is captured by the veins before it can reach the body surface and is returned to the deep body.

As a means of keeping warm, seals and porpoises "live faster" than most land mammals. Their metabolic rate is higher. Metabolism is the heat-producing activity which goes on in all body cells.

But the largest whales may have a problem keeping *cool*. Heat conservation in a harbor porpoise is surely a different matter from that in a blue whale which is 2,000 times heavier—100 pounds compared to 100 tons. Though no one has yet been able to measure the metabolic rate of a large, healthy whale, it is thought to be only one-half that of a sloth—a sluggish land mammal. One-half of the blubber of a large whale could theoretically keep the animal going at its basal metabolic rate for four months.

Seals, as well as whales, can suffer from too much heat. On a sunny day, they will wave their flippers or pant with open mouth like a dog, or throw sand on their back, or go for a swim. Seals often seem to weep in hot weather. Because they have no duct between the eyes and nose, their tears spill down their cheeks.

The Challenge of a Fluid Habitat

Marine mammals are completely at home in their fluid habitat. They feel and respond to the water as a person feels and responds to the ground beneath his feet or to the wind against his face. When the first

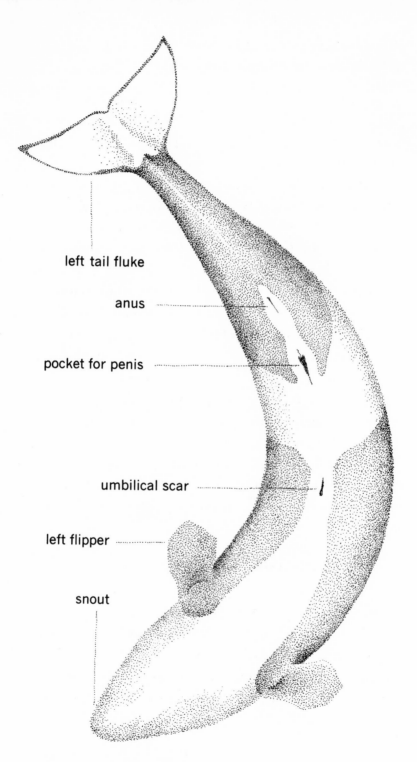

left tail fluke

anus

pocket for penis

umbilical scar

left flipper

snout

Figure 19   Killer whale

ancient marine mammals learned to hunt in the sea, nature molded their bodies into sleek and streamlined shapes. Legs disappeared or became shortened. Sex organs and nipples withdrew partly or completely into pockets. Modern marine mammals have eyelids but no eyelashes; most of them have few or no claws. In the cetaceans, the neck bones were gradually telescoped or jammed together, which allowed the body to approach more nearly the shape of a swift-moving torpedo.

Sea otters usually feed in shallow forests of kelp; they move rather slowly. When chased by a power boat, they can swim 5 or 6 miles per hour. Strangely, they swim faster belly-upward, forelegs held at the sides, webbed hind feet pumping the water.

When frightened, a fur seal can course through the water at about 10 miles per hour, swimming with powerful breast strokes. A trained California sea lion will gain enough exit speed to hurdle a bar more than 7 feet above the water.

Sirenians are sluggish and heavy-boned, yet in a short burst of speed, a manatee can swim 15 miles per hour.

Of all the marine mammals, the killer whale—the predator supreme—is the fastest swimmer. An officer of the steamship *Monterey* traveling at 24 miles per hour saw a killer approach the ship at an estimated speed of 34 miles per hour. Hawaiian scientists clocked a spotted porpoise at a top speed of 27 miles per hour. Whiteside porpoises in a California oceanarium were trained to leap in unison, four together, as high as 15 feet above the water. Skana, a killer whale in the Vancouver Public Aquarium, leaps on command to touch a goal 23 feet above her pool.

Swimming at a speed of 10 miles per hour, a large blue whale develops 45 horsepower, or about the power of a compact automobile. It would be interesting to know how much power is developed by a humpback whale when, during courtship or play, it hurls its many-ton body completely out of the sea.

The Challenge of Three Dimensions

Though most land mammals spend their lives in horizontal space only, marine mammals move also in vertical space—up and down in the sea, locating food and dodging enemies which may rush in from any side. Men, too, have begun experimentally to live in the sea. Riding on submarine sleds and breathing air from tanks, they now penetrate the haunts of the creatures of the deep. Before the scientific discoveries of the twentieth century, men wondered how some marine mammals are able to dive to depths of over one-half mile and stay under for more than an hour. They wondered, especially, how marine mammals avoid the "bends," that painful and sometimes fatal condition which a human diver suffers when he rises too quickly to the surface, and which results from bubbles of nitrogen gas coming out of solution in his blood.

During the dive of a marine mammal, the heartbeat slows to as little as one-tenth its usual rate. Body temperature and metabolic rate drop. Blood leaves the extremities while continuing to supply the heart and brain—the organs of prime need. Marine mammals can store more oxygen in their blood and in their muscles than can most land mammals. And in seals (but not in cetaceans) the amount of blood relative to the weight of the body is one and a half to two times greater than that of humans. In a full-grown walrus the forked veins which drain the lower body are so enormous that a man can draw them over his legs like a pair of pants!

Marine mammals can tolerate high levels of carbon dioxide, which is the gas that makes a person panic when he holds his breath too long. They can also tolerate high levels of lactic acid, a breakdown product of muscle activity. Their muscles can continue to propel their bodies through the sea long after a land mammal will have collapsed from exhaustion.

They have an automatic cutoff system involving nerves and muscles which keeps them from trying to breathe if they are temporarily stunned while under water. A marine mammal found dead on the bottom of its pool may have suffocated but will not have drowned; its lungs will not be full of water.

The source of bends in the human diver is nitrogen in the air which he continuously breathes from a tank. But the marine mammal has only to contend with the nitrogen in the one lungful of air which it inhales

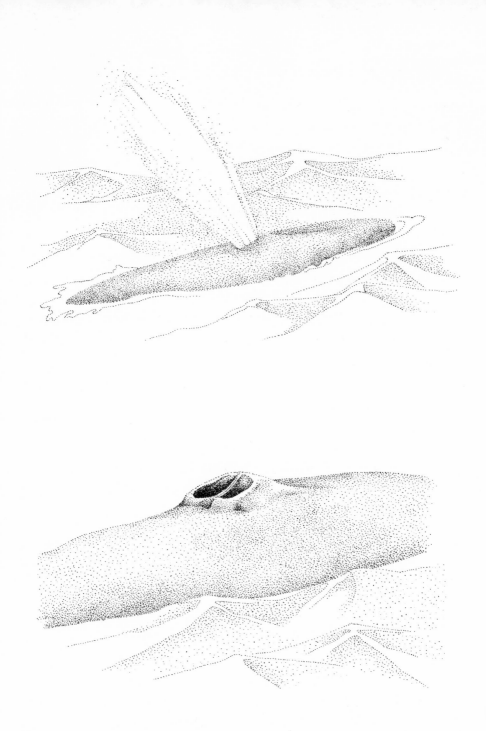

Figure 20 Blowholes of a baleen whale during and after a blow

before diving. Moreover, when a seal or cetacean dives deeply, the lung collapses and its contained gases move into nonabsorptive passages within the head and neck.

All cetaceans periodically "blow" or exhale forcibly at the surface of the water. The toothed cetaceans have one blowhole (nostril), the baleen cetaceans two. A fast-moving porpoise will blow and take a new breath within less than a second's time. This feat was explained when zoologists found that gases in the blow of a gray whale move at 400 miles per hour!

How can anyone know the maximum depth of dive of a marine mammal? Because sea otters habitually feed in water less than 180 feet deep, and walruses in water less than 240 feet deep, it is assumed that these species have no urge to go deeper. (However, a dead sea otter was recently found in an Alaskan crab trap on the bottom in 318 feet of water.) Sirenians also stay in the upper, sunlit waters among the green plants upon which they feed.

A team of physiologists once fastened a depth recorder around the neck of a Weddell seal and found that the animal could dive to 1,968 feet and could remain submerged for up to 70 minutes. First, the men sawed a hole through 6 feet of sea ice. Then they caught a seal, fastened a recorder to it, and released the seal beside the hole. When it later returned to the hole for air, they removed the instrument and read its message, which had been inscribed by a moving needle on a smoked-glass disk.

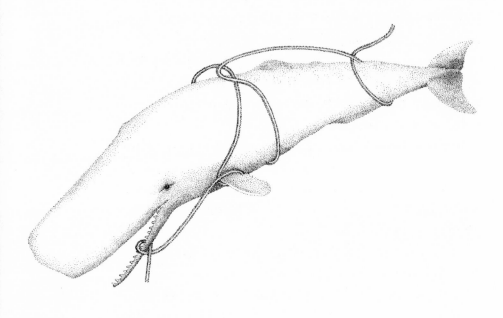

Figure 21   Sperm whale tangled in a deep sea cable

Radio-tracked porpoises in the wild have dived to 600 feet. At least one tame one, a bottlenose, was trained to dive on command to 1,000 feet.

The marine mammal record for deep diving is held by an unfortunate sperm whale whose body was found tangled in a cable 3,720 feet, or more than half a mile, below the surface. A killer whale was found tangled at 3,318 feet and a humpback at 390 feet.

The whalemen of the nineteenth century claimed that a harpooned and frightened bottlenose whale would stay down for as long as two hours. Perhaps so. Nowadays, the length of its dive could not be tested in the same manner, for the modern whaling harpoon carries a bomb in its head.

In the boundless, ever-changing sea, whales and porpoises have found survival value in a behavior known as care giving or mutual aid. Because it resembles human kindness, it endears those animals to people. There are many stories about cetacean mothers, or even "aunties," protecting an injured calf. There are other stories about adult whales standing by, or physically supporting, one another in time of trouble.

Two men were collecting live fish off the Florida coast by the use of small, but stunning, charges of dynamite. Suddenly they saw two porpoises swimming slowly and supporting a third one which had been stunned. The two porpoises held the injured one to the surface where it could breathe. After several minutes it recovered, and all three took off at high speed.

Now that scientists know how strong the care-giving instinct can be, they understand stories of porpoises saving humans. One woman reported that on an occasion when she was swimming in the surf, she was tumbled by waves and feared that she was drown-

Figure 22   Two porpoises supporting an injured companion

ing. Suddenly she felt a tremendous shove. She came to her senses on the beach. A man ran up to her and said that he had seen a porpoise pushing what he thought was her dead body!

But porpoises are *not* meek and loving. In captivity, at least, they are often aggressive toward one another. Their aggression is a kind of law enforcement which maintains the structure of porpoise society. It keeps individuals in their places and it safeguards individuals' property rights to food.

The Challenge of Salt

Persons who work at oceanariums often hear the question: Do cetaceans drink? A team of scientists decided to find out. They placed a pilot whale, a bottlenose porpoise, and a whiteside porpoise in a tank of sea water containing a harmless radioactive tracer (sodium-24). At 2-hour intervals, they collected and analyzed samples of urine, blood, and "tears" from the animals. They found that the tracer content of the body fluids rose steadily. The animals were indeed drinking sea water. However, the team could not tell whether the animals were drinking for the water, or for the salt, or simply because they could not help swallowing water. Anyway, the water did not make them sick, as it would have affected a person.

The tongue of the bottlenose porpoise has many peculiar mucous glands. Their secretion may possibly serve to rid the blood of excess salt. Here is a challenging problem for future scientists.

The more that is learned about the abilities of sea mammals to tolerate salt, the more likely it seems that the "problem" of saltiness is not real. Mice which normally live in salt marshes can be held in the laboratory for months on end on a diet of dry food and sea water. Mice and ground squirrels of the desert remain healthy during long dry spells without any water at all.

However, all animals which do not drink must manufacture water within their bodies. This so-called water of metabolism is derived from the chemical burning of food products in the bloodstream, a form of oxidation which releases carbon dioxide and water. The fat stores of marine mammals are an especially rich source of metabolic water.

One reason for suspecting that salt water does not bother marine mammals is that some species move freely in the wild between freshwater streams and the ocean. Their kidneys adjust to the difference in salinity. The harbor seal, manatee, beluga, and several species of porpoises in South America, Asia, and Africa, are equally at home in salt water or fresh.

In Lake Baikal, Siberia, about 30,000 ringed seals are born, live, and die in fresh water. The Chinese lake porpoise and the Amazon porpoise are likewise locked for life in freshwater systems.

4. FOOD PREFERENCE

Marine mammals have only one diagnostic feature —one unique habit—which sets them apart from all other mammals: they depend for food on plants or animals obtained beneath the surface of the sea. There are a few exceptions to this habit. Now and then a "rogue" walrus will feed on carrion flesh on the shore. Sea lions and leopard seals will leave the water in order to grab seal pups or birds from the beach. A porpoise observed by a man in Georgia slid completely out of water onto a soft mudbank in order to catch small fish trapped in its bow wave.

They store food as body fat, never in caches or hoards. A female gray whale, weighing 24 tons at the peak of her feeding season, may weigh only 16 tons after she has finished her winter migration and has given birth to a calf. The loss will have been largely in fat.

A curious feature of the digestive system in some marine mammals is the very long intestine. That of one bull elephant seal measured 662 feet. In sperm whales, the gut is about 500 feet long during life and 1,200 feet long after death (stretched on the ground). There is no good explanation for intestines of such length.

The stomach in cetaceans is divided into four or more chambers. The first is a muscular "gizzard," the others are digestive pouches. This partitioning resembles that of the ruminants (cattle, sheep, and their relatives), the mammals which are believed to share with whales a common land ancestor.

Sea otters, seals, and several kinds of cetaceans commonly swallow stones. The stomach of a California sea lion contained 60 pounds of stones; that of a pilot whale, a single rock weighing 21 pounds. Whatever may be the impulse that leads marine mammals to swallow stones, it is surely not—as an old sailor's yarn would have it—for ballast!

The variety of foods eaten by one or another marine mammal is very wide. The food variety can be compared with that of bats—those other mammals which also live in a three-dimensional world, though one of air rather than of water. Some bats eat insects; others eat fish, fruit, nectar, or fresh blood. For each kind of bat, the teeth, shape of the mouth, and chemistry of the digestive juices are tailored to fit its diet. So also with the marine mammal species.

Marine mammal foods can be categorized as four diets: fish, squid, and shellfish; warm-blooded prey; plankton; and sea grasses. Few of the marine mammals eat from only one of these diets; there is overlap. When a baleen whale, which ordinarily depends upon plankton food, happens upon a school of small fish, it devours them. During its puppy weeks, a harp seal will eat many plankton organisms which, as an adult, it will pass by because of their small size.

Fish, Squid, and Shellfish

Of those marine mammals which eat fish, squid, and shellfish, some habitually feed near the bottom while others feed in the upper waters.

The massive, crushing teeth of the sea otter show that it eats many rough, hard-shelled, and spiny foods obtained from the sea floor. A scientist examined the stomachs of about three hundred Alaskan sea otters and found fish, 50 percent; mollusks (clams, snails, and chitons), 37 percent; sea urchins and starfish, 11 percent; sea worms, crabs, shrimps, and other forms, 2 percent.

The sea otter is the only nonprimate mammal known regularly to use a tool. While floating belly up at the surface, it devours whatever it has pried loose from the bottom. It often places a flat stone on its chest and uses this as an anvil against which to break clams, sea urchins, or crabs. Susie, a sea otter in the Seattle Zoo, liked to pound clams against the concrete wall of her tank. Her keeper obligingly gave her a rock, which she promptly used to demolish the edge of the tank!

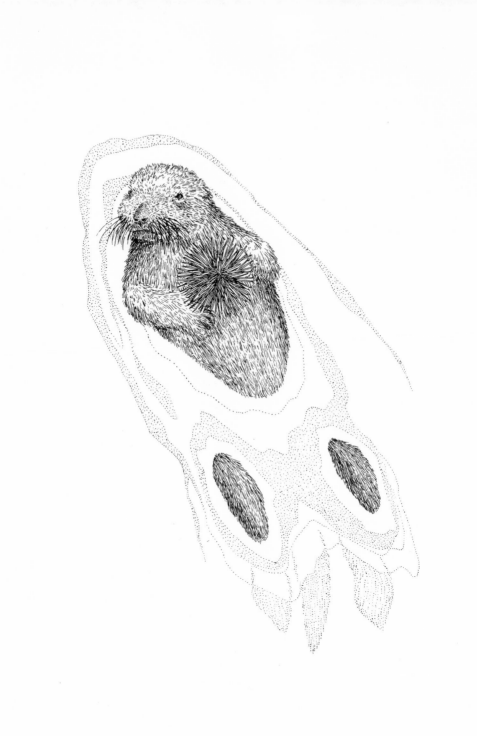

Figure 23   Sea otter feeding on a sea urchin

Food Preference

In relation to its size, the sea otter is perhaps the most voracious of all marine mammals. Susie daily ate nearly 9 pounds of fish, squid, and clam-meat, amounting to one-quarter of her body weight.

The harbor seal and the walrus, both of which inhabit shallow water, depend heavily upon bottom animals for food. Scientists once believed that the walrus digs clams with its tusks; now they know that it loosens them from the mud with its strong sucking lips and whiskers. Having no hands, it cannot hold a clam, but it can neatly suck out the meat while leaving the shell behind. Its mouth and tongue are a powerful vacuum cleaner.

The blind river porpoise of India, surprisingly, feeds by swimming on its side, rather than on its belly like a proper porpoise. It trails one flipper along the bottom as though feeling its way.

Most of the marine mammals of the world are adapted for feeding in open water, for the open sea is far more productive in total biomass than is the narrow coastal zone. About ten thousand kinds of fish and squid live in the open sea.

The squid is a mainstay food. It is related to the octopus; both are soft-bodied mollusks lacking a shell. Squids of one kind or another live in all the seas of the world and are far more numerous than is generally known. The largest is the deep-sea giant squid, *Architeuthis*, which, including its tentacles, or "arms," is more than 60 feet long.

The teeth of the fur seals are sharp, conical, and closely set, forming an efficient trap for catching small schooling fish like herring, and for holding slippery squid. When a seal catches a small fish, it simply gulps it down whole. When it catches a larger one, such as a cod or rockfish, it carries it to the surface and shakes it vigorously, breaking it into bite-size pieces. Gulls often rest on the water near a feeding seal, hoping for scattered scraps. More than a hundred kinds of fish and squid have been identified in Alaskan fur seal stomachs.

Porpoises may work together as a team to herd mullet and other schooling fishes into a tight ball where individuals can easily be caught. A porpoise usually seizes its prey head-first and swallows it whole.

Two men in a boat off California watched an attack by several hundred harbor porpoises, thirty to fifty sea lions, and several thousand gulls. All were feeding on a great school of sardines moving just beneath the surface. Repeatedly, from five to seven porpoises would form a rank, side by side, and charge madly through the school. One porpoise might eat as many as a dozen fish in a rush. Other porpoises circled the school continuously, as though they were watch-dogs.

Porpoises pursue and eat a wide variety of shrimps and swimming crabs. A biologist who harpooned three bottlenose porpoises off a Texas shore found nearly two gallons of shrimp in their stomachs. He washed the shrimp and ate them!

Food Preference

The largest of all fish-and-squid eaters is the 60-ton sperm whale. Though it has useful teeth only in its lower jaw, it tackles the giant squid in the absolute darkness of the ocean's depths. Workers at a whaling station, while cutting open the stomach of a sperm whale, found squid remains weighing 405 pounds. The skin of every old sperm whale carries scars left by the sharp beaks and rasping tentacles of squid. The sperm whale, like most animals, is a food opportunist. In the stomach of one big male there were found a partly digested shark over 10 feet long, the skin of a seal, and 8 feet of fishing line with six hooks.

Now and then commercial fishermen try to have laws passed to permit the killing of seals or sea otters. They claim—with some justice—that seals are competitors for fish and that sea otters are competitors for abalones and clams. Indeed, the northern fur seals collectively eat nearly a million tons of food per year. But the ecology of the sea is unbelievably complex. When a seal removes a fish from a marine community of thousands of different organisms, what sort of ecologic "hole" has it left? When a sea otter takes an abalone, its act may or may not prevent an abalone of similar size from reaching the table of some human family.

Friends of the California sea otter point out that, while these animals may seem to be hurting a shellfish industry worth several million dollars a year, they are helping a seaweed industry worth about fifty million. That is, the otters feed on sea urchins which otherwise would have fed on seaweed. The California sea otter

53

population poses some very difficult problems in wildlife management.

The stomachs of sea lions killed near the mouth of the Klamath River in California during a salmon run contained no salmon but were packed with lampreys. The lamprey is a parasitic fish which attaches to salmon and sucks the blood from them. The real effect of sea lions upon the salmon industry is hard to determine.

It is a different matter when individual seals learn to rob nets or lines. Here they can cause serious damage, both to the fish catch and to the gear. Fishermen are justified in killing nuisance individuals in commercial fishing waters, which is not the same thing as the wholesale killing of animals which, along with people, deserve a share of the riches of the sea.

Warm-blooded Prey

Of all the marine mammals, only the killer whale and leopard seal habitually feed on birds and mammals. These predators can be called the wolf and the tiger of the sea. The rest of the marine mammals depend on cold-blooded prey.

Many stories are told of the "vicious" killer whale, whose mouth gleams with forty to fifty teeth the size of carrots. The beast is said to enjoy rending the flesh of seals, porpoises, whales, and humans. In Norwegian, its name is *spekkhoggeren,* or fat-chopper. But Japanese whalemen who examined the stomachs of more than three hundred killers found a wide variety of food remains. They were (in this order): fishes (cod, flatfish, sardine, salmon, tuna, and others), squid and octopus, porpoises, whales, and seals. In the stomachs of ten killers taken along the Pacific coast of North America were found the remains of at least seven sea lions, seven elephant seals, four porpoises, and one minke whale, as well as fish and squid.

There is no authentic record of an attack by a killer whale upon man. H. G. Ponting, British photographer of the Scott party to the South Pole in 1911, thought that he might have been an intended victim. In *Scott's Last Voyage* * he wrote: "I had got to within six feet of the edge of the [sea] ice—which was about a yard thick—when to my consternation it suddenly heaved up under my feet and split into fragments around me; whilst the eight whales, lined up side by side and almost touching each other burst from under the ice and blew off steam. The head of one was within two yards of me. I saw its nostrils open, and at such close quarters the release of its pent-up breath was like a blast from an air-compressor. The noise of the eight simultaneous blows sounded terrific, and I was enveloped in the warm vapour of the nearest 'spout,' which had a strong fishy smell."

* Full documentation for quotations in text is given in the bibliography, in alphabetical order by name of author or editor.

Did the killers take Ponting for a seal which they could tip into the water and devour? We shall never know.

What is known about the biology of the killer whale has mainly been learned since 1964. In that year, collectors for the Vancouver Public Aquarium succeeded in holding a live specimen, Moby Doll (actually a male), in captivity for three months. He proved to be so fascinating that efforts were made to capture others. To date, about three hundred killer whales have been netted alive in the enclosed waters of southern British Columbia (Canada) and northern Puget Sound (Washington). Some have been shipped by air to oceanariums as far away as Europe. Moby Doll fasted for fifty-four days before he accepted food. Then he ate 100 to 200 pounds of fish daily until he died a month later of a wound sustained during his capture.

Strangely, porpoises can safely be kept in the same pool with killer whales. The killers do not attack them, and even seem to enjoy their company. This tolerance illustrates a well-known predator-prey relationship among mammals. The predator is programmed by instinct to follow a scenario which goes something like this: hunger—chase—frenzy of attack—quiet devouring of prey. But in the unnatural situation of a pool, the triggering impulses of hunger and open-sea chase are never fired; the killer is never motivated to attack a porpoise.

Food Preference

There is still no proof that large whales in good health in the open sea are harmed by killer whales. How they defend themselves is unclear. However, killers are quick to attack a crippled whale or one trapped by low tide in a small, shallow bay. Canadian biologists happened upon an attack by seven killers upon a minke whale trapped in shallow water. It took the attackers nearly an hour to kill the whale. Most of the action took place under water; probably the whale died of suffocation after it had lost a great deal of blood. From time to time, large chunks of flesh and blobs of oil would rise to the surface. On the following day, the men found the body of the victim, neatly skinned and lacking its tongue but with the rest of its body intact. A Norwegian whaleman once harpooned, but did not kill, a bottlenose whale. Suddenly, three killers swam in and began to bite at the flippers and tail flukes of the wounded animal. The man hauled in the bottlenose, now near death, and finished it off.

A man in a boat off the California coast once saw a big male killer leap clear of the water holding a full-grown sea lion crosswise in its jaws! While a scientist was watching a killer whale chase a sea lion in the rocky shallows of the California coast, the frightened seal suddenly changed its course and the killer smashed headfirst into a large rock. It lay there for ten minutes, stunned and quivering, before it recovered and swam away.

Killer whales commonly hunt in packs of 3 to 20;

an average group will contain 10. For reasons yet unknown, packs occasionally join to make a group of 100
or more individuals.

The leopard seal of the Antarctic, the other marine mammal that habitually feeds on warm-blooded
prey, is an agile beast weighing up to a thousand
pounds, with a long "reptilian" neck and sharp, re-
curved teeth. Its peculiar trachea (windpipe) can
collapse to ease the swallowing of large-bodied birds.
About 150,000 leopard seals live in the pack ice of
Antarctica. During past geologic ages leopard seals co-
evolved with penguins, those flightless birds which
abound in millions in southern waters and upon which
the seals feed. The predators also attack other aquatic
birds, as well as fish, squid, and an occasional seal of a
different species. The leopard seal has no counterpart
in Arctic waters where flightless birds are lacking.

The leopard seal is a solitary hunter. It patrols the
ice front, alert for penguins which must leave their
rookeries daily to feed in the sea. The seals and the
penguins probably spend more than half their lives in
icy water. A seal usually grabs a bird under water,
though it may also rise under thin ice, breaking the ice
and knocking the bird into the water. Sometimes a bird
being chased in the water will escape by taking a zig-
zag course or by leaping 6 to 8 feet to the safety of
overhanging sea ice. Or a seal may chase a bird on top
of the ice. Once it has the bird in its mouth, it bites and
shakes it literally out of its skin, then swallows the

body. Even so, it is a poor skinner, for its droppings are characteristically full of feathers.

Whalemen saw a leopard seal slashing at the dead body of a whale, tearing off large chunks of flesh by rotary movements of its jaws and teeth. Leopard seals will occasionally grab and devour the pups of Weddell and crabeater seals.

Plankton Food

Plankton is the collective name for the motley mixture of very small plant and animal organisms that drift or swim feebly in oceans, rivers, and lakes. Whalemen call the marine plankton krill (a word both singular and plural). They see it often as a vast, reddish stain on the surface of the ocean. It is made up of hundreds of species, including microscopic plants, tiny crustaceans, jellyfish, arrow worms, and the eggs and young of fishes and shellfishes. The most conspicuous organisms in the krill are species of shrimplike euphasids up to 2 inches long.

The world ocean contains an incredible amount of krill, estimated at between 500 million and 5 billion tons. If it could be harvested, it would yield perhaps 100 million tons a year, equivalent to the present world harvest of fish and shellfish. Only a minute fraction of the krill stock is now being harvested, and only by

Japanese and Soviet experimental fishery biologists.

Plankton is the main food supply of the baleen whales. These will also take mouthfuls of water laden with small, sardine-like fishes. During the early evolution of the mouth in baleen whales, fleshy ridges on the upper gum gradually took over the function of teeth. The ridges became a series of horny plates. In modern species, the plates are used for filtering plankton food. In the bowhead whale, where baleen reaches its greatest development, the plates number 350 or more on each side of the mouth, some of them over 12 feet long.

A Japanese scientist measured the filtering surface of the baleen of a sei whale; it was 38 square feet. Thus, every time a sei whale pushes its tongue against the roof of its mouth, squishing out a broth of krill and water through its baleen, it is in effect casting a net about the size of a "king size," 6-by-6-foot bed.

In some ways the most peculiar of the baleen species is the gray whale, which lives in coastal waters of the North Pacific Ocean and adjacent seas. Though it feeds on krill, it also scoops up small crustaceans, worms, and other boneless animals that live in, or just above, the bottom mud. It is often seen rising to the surface with mud streaming from its snout and baleen.

No one has yet tried to hold a full-grown baleen whale in an oceanarium. The Japanese have kept young minke whales alive for short periods of time. In a California aquarium, a baby gray whale was a welcome guest until it began to eat chopped fish and squid

Individual krill

Figure 24   Baleen whale engulfing krill

worth $200 a day. Then its keepers turned it loose in the Pacific Ocean.

Two kinds of seals depend heavily on krill—the crabeater seal of the Antarctic and the little ringed seal of the Arctic. When explorers first discovered the crabeater, they named it for the reddish fragments, supposedly of crabs, which always color its droppings on the ice. Actually, the fragments are the shells of euphausids.

Nature has carved the teeth of the crabeater into fantastic shapes, the better to adapt them for straining krill. Judith E. King, seal expert of the British Museum, wrote in *Seals of the World* that the crabeater catches krill "by swimming into a shoal of them with open mouth, probably sucking them in, and then sieving the krill from the water through the spaces between the cusps [points] of the complicated check teeth."

In view of the richness and abundance of their food supply, it is not surprising that crabeaters are the most numerous of all seals. Their population is estimated at 10 million or more.

Because of their remoteness from civilization, crabeaters have never been hunted commercially. Some businessmen argue that they should be exploited for meat, oil, and skins. Most scientists, on the other hand, feel that the whole Antarctic region and its diversity of life forms should be held in trust for mankind as a sort of perpetual museum of research and education.

Food Preference

The second most numerous seal in the world is the ringed seal, with a population of about 5 million. Like the crabeater, it is plentiful because it feeds at a low level of the food ladder of the sea. The food ladder, or food chain, is imaginary. It describes a series of eater-and-eaten dependencies. About 1,000 pounds of plant plankton at the bottom of the ladder supports 100 pounds of animal plankton, which supports 10 pounds of baleen whale, which supports 1 pound of top predator, be it killer whale or whaleman.

Most ringed seals live at the edge of sea ice around the Arctic Ocean and, in open water leads, to the North Pole itself. Several populations live in lakes. For centuries, the coastal Eskimos have depended on ringed seals for food, clothing, and fuel oil.

Though the ringed seal filters krill through its delicate teeth, it also captures fish shorter than about eight inches, and shellfish. In a sample of 1,432 stomachs, food remains were identified as fish (Arctic cod, sculpins, saffron cod, and sandlance) and crustaceans (shrimp, krill, and crabs). During the annual spring "bloom" of plankton, krill is often the only food taken.

Sea Grasses

Among the marine mammals, only the sirenians are vegetarians. They graze on submarine pastures of tropical plants known locally as turtle grass, manatee

grass, or dugong grass. These plants are not seaweeds (algae) but flowering plants similar to the eel
grass which grows in bright green ribbons in the tidal
zones of North America. Manatees feed both in freshwater streams and in coastal marine waters; dugongs
mainly in coastal marine waters.

Manatees are voracious feeders; they browse
steadily on whatever plants they can find. Their gro-
tesque, fleshy, muscular lips, armed with bristles, serve
in place of hands for moving food into the mouth.
There the food is chewed by stout grinding teeth. If a
manatee is very hungry, it will half wallow, half swim,
up the slope of a stream bank, though it will never leave
the water entirely. On land it is helpless. In captivity it
may eat 30 to 50 pounds of assorted vegetables a day.

Manatees are being used to control the growth of
weeds in tropical canals. Here such weeds as water
hyacinth (*Eichornia*), salvinia (*Salvinia*), and water
lettuce (*Pistia*) grow rapidly. They choke canals which
are needed for navigation, for generating electric
power, for fishing, for irrigation, and for draining farm-
lands. In Florida alone, the cost of controlling water
weeds is over $15 million a year. Some zoologists be-
lieve that, where manatees can be moved to such
canals, they will keep the weeds down to acceptable
levels.

There lived into historic time another sirenian, the
Steller sea cow, about which little is known. It was
seen alive by one naturalist, Georg Wilhelm Steller,
a German-born Russian. He described it from field

Figure 25 Manatee feeding on sea grass

notes made on Bering Island, off the coast of Kamchatka, in 1741–1742. Steller died on the return trip to Russia, and by 1768 the last sea cow on earth had been killed by hunters. As judged from Steller's notes and from skeletons later dug from the sands of Bering Island, the largest sea cow weighed 7 tons and was 25 feet long. It had no teeth; it fed by crushing seaweeds with its bristly lips, tongue, and hard palate.

5. EVOLUTION
OF SENSES

In their submarine surroundings, marine mammals depend on vibrations of the water—sound and ultrasound—to communicate with one another and to receive information about objects which they cannot see. All of them have hearing organs, though only the sea otter and the walking seals have external ears. Sea otters and all seals feel vibrations through their sensitive whiskers. If blinded by accident, they are still able to feed and stay fairly healthy. A few kinds of whales have coarse hairs along the underbody, though these are more sensitive to water currents than to sound. They act as speedometers.

While marine mammals were gaining powers of hearing, they were losing powers of smell and taste. The sense of smell is still keen in the sea otter but is progressively fainter in seals, sirenians, and cetaceans. Sea-otter hunters try to approach their prey upwind so as not to alarm it. Porpoises evidently have poor senses of smell and taste; their olfactory brain lobes (which respond to smell) have almost disappeared, and taste buds on the tongue are sparsely scattered.

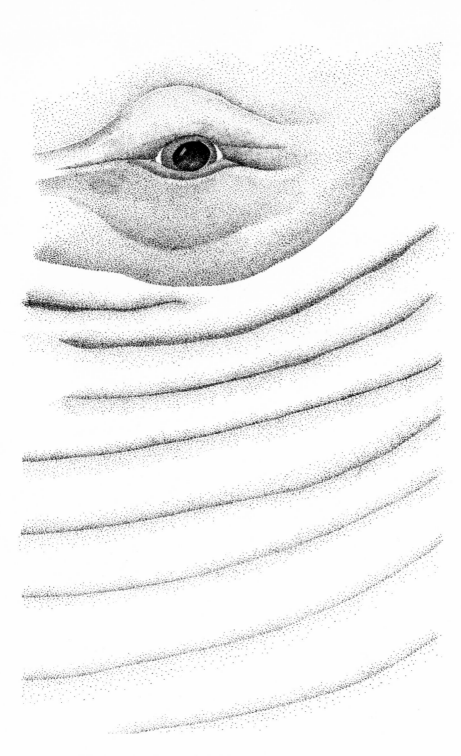

Figure 26   Eye of whale

Evolution of Senses

The evolution of sight in marine mammals has followed an irregular path. The eyes of the sea otter, sirenians, and cetaceans are small; the eyes of seals (except walruses) are large. Marine mammals in general can see much better under water than in air, and they can see very well in dim light.

Some seals feed at night by approaching their prey from beneath, silhouetting it against the sky. In the laboratory, tame sea lions can identify target shapes and patterns of elaborate design. Their ability to discriminate suggests that they can also quickly select their favorite food fishes in the open sea.

Roughly in order of their dependence on land, marine mammals produce sounds (vocalize) in the open air. Members of the most completely aquatic groups—the toothed and baleen cetaceans—almost never vocalize in air. The elephant seals, sea lions, and fur seals, all of which breed in large social groups, are the noisiest. The "ballpark" racket of a fur seal rookery can be heard for over a mile, as can the booming, pile-driver sound of a bull elephant seal in the mating season. A young sea otter, separated from its mother, will cry *"waah . . . waah"*; a young harbor seal, *"kroo . . . kroo."* Karl W. Kenyon, an American scientist who spent many hours watching sea otters in Alaska and in captivity, says that they scream, whine, coo, snarl, hiss, grunt, and bark (*The Sea Otter in the Eastern North Pacific*).

Among the most beautiful songs of any marine mammals are those of cetaceans vocalizing under

water. Early efforts to describe in words their rich
vocabularies have given way to the use of voice prints,
or sonagrams. Sounds are converted through instrument to squiggly lines on a strip of paper. A voice print
can correct for tone deafness (sense of pitch) in the
human observer and it can also record ultrasounds
which lie far outside the range of any human ear.
Cetaceans may vocalize at rates as low as 20 beats per
second, producing a sound like the slow creak of a
rusty hinge, or as high as 256,000 beats. The sharpest
human ear cannot detect sounds shriller than 20,000
beats.

Porpoises can tell apart the individual voices of
their companions, while elephant seals on different
islands can speak to one another in separate island
dialects. Even porpoises of unrelated species seem to
understand a few of one another's words. When the
recorded distress call of a bottlenose porpoise was
played under water, it threw nearby spinner porpoises
into panic.

Scientists who listened to the voice of a blue
whale off the coast of South America measured the
volume of the sound. They were astonished. It was,
they said, the most powerful of all known animal
voices and would surely carry under water for a hundred miles.

Some underwater sounds, like the submarine
barking of sea lions and the whistling of belugas, can
be heard clearly above water by a person in a boat.
Whalemen used to call the beluga the "sea canary."

Evolution of Senses

Cetaceans produce three main kinds of sounds. *Echo-locating clicks* reflect from objects and help the animal explore its environment. A sound which resembles a click-train can be produced by running one's thumbnail quickly down the teeth of a comb. *Voices* resemble the barks, squeals, and other calls of land mammals. These are associated with emotional states which, to humans at least, call for displays of anger, threat, alarm, hunger, or sympathy. One can imitate a porpoise squeal by sounding off in one's throat with mouth closed and nostrils pinched together. *Whistles* are pure tones unlike any sounds made by land mammals except humans—and possibly the "whistling" marmots of the Rocky Mountains. The purpose of whistle tones is uncertain; many cetaceans do not make them. When the whistle sweeps a wide frequency range—that is, changes pitch—very quickly and then stops, it is called a *chirp*.

Echo-location in porpoises was discovered in the 1950s. A collector for a Florida aquarium wondered how porpoises in the open sea could find, as they often did, ways to escape from his net. He was puzzled, for he was netting in the darkness of night. How could the animals "see" the net?

A Florida zoologist took up the challenge; he tested a porpoise in a tank of muddy water. He offered it two kinds of fish, one of which it preferred over the other. Somehow, even from a distance, the porpoise would instantly choose, and swim toward, the tastier fish. Each time that it was asked to choose it gave voice to a click-train. These clicks, the scientist concluded, were telling the animal all that it needed to know about the location, the shape, and even the texture (hardness or softness) of the fish.

Only porpoises among the marine mammals are known to echo-locate, though it is likely that other toothed cetaceans do also. Whether baleen whales, sirenians, seals, and the sea otter can echo-locate has not been proved. However, all are known to give voice to underwater sounds, and some of the sounds are of the kind that *could* serve for echo-location.

The people who train seals and cetaceans to do tricks or to carry out research duties use underwater sounds as commands. A mathematician has invented a machine which translates human words into underwater whistles which a porpoise seems to understand and to which it responds. On voice command, individual porpoises are called to perform certain tasks. Sometimes the command word is hidden in a long sentence, yet the porpoise can recognize it.

Elvar, a porpoise trained in a Miami pool, had a natural talent for mimicry. After several years he learned to say, in a reasonable imitation of English, "All right, let's go!" No thoughtful person would claim, however, that Elvar knew what he was saying.

Little is known of the anatomy of sound production in those marine mammals which lack vocal cords —the sirenians and cetaceans. In the bottlenose porpoise, sound evidently comes from a sort of Adam's apple deep in the throat. Cetaceans also communicate by slapping the water with their tails—an act known as lobtailing—or with their whole bodies. The smashing sounds which result can be impressive.

Playbacks of recorded sounds of killer whales have been used to frighten beluga whales, which are predators upon fish, out of valuable salmon rivers. The sounds have also been used to chase porpoises away from tuna nets where the mammals are apt to get tangled and suffocate.

The Greenland Eskimos employ a trick for luring belugas close to a boat where a harpooner can strike them. They stick a 4-foot length of iron pipe into the water next to the hull of the boat and make sounds like a hurt baby whale into the open end of the pipe.

6. MEASUREMENTS OF INTELLIGENCE

We humans like to believe that at least a few other animals on earth are intelligent, for in so believing we feel somehow less alone. Unfortunately, intelligence is hard to define. For ordinary purposes, it may be thought of as a blend of the abilities to behave outside the rigid bounds of instinct, to learn through trial and error and by watching others, to communicate in elaborate sounds and gestures, to care for associates in distress, and to play. These abilities add up to a sort of total awareness and freedom which we associate with men and porpoises and to lesser degrees with whales, sirenians, seals, and sea otters.

What does *play* have to do with intelligence? Dr. Sterling Bunnell, a California psychiatrist, wrote: "Extreme playfulness and humor are conspicuous in dolphins. . . . Despite its low status in puritanical value systems, play is a hallmark of intelligence and is indispensable for creativity and flexibility. Its marked development in cetaceans makes it likely that they will frolic with their minds as much as with their bodies" (in McIntyre, ed., *Mind in the Waters*).

Figure 27   Trained fur seal

A *Natural History of Marine Mammals*

Karen Pryor, a student of animal behavior who lives in Hawaii and has spent many days watching small cetaceans in captivity, wrote: "A group of spinning porpoises make delightful shy and gentle swimming companions and will harmlessly play with a human swimmer for half an hour at a time, drifting into the swimmer's arms, swirling around him, and pacing every human movement with their own kind of . . . water ballet" ("Behavior and Learning in Porpoises and Whales").

It is hard to decide, simply by watching an animal's behavior, whether it is smart. But there is another approach—studying the size and structure of its brain. A brain is a computer having trillions of connecting links. One can argue that the larger the brain, the smarter the animal. The catch in this reasoning is that any large mammal, regardless of its intelligence, must have a large brain if only to match the great mass of its body tissues and organs.

Well, then why not divide brain weight by body weight to rule out the effect of body size and leave a clear index of intelligence? The table on page 77 shows the brain weights, and the ratio of each to body weight, for eleven species of cetaceans. In the largest one—the blue whale—the brain makes up only $\frac{1}{5000}$ of 1 percent of the body weight, while in the smallest ones—the porpoises—it makes up over 1 percent. Moreover, in this kind of arrangement, the brain of man seems to rank only slightly above that of the

narwhal! Obviously, brain-to-body ratio is not a good
index of "braininess."

Brain Weight and Body Weight in Cetaceans and Humans

	Brain weight (pounds)	Body weight (pounds)	Brain weight as percentage of body weight
BALEEN CETACEANS			
Humpback whale	16.5	90,000	0.018
Blue whale	14.3	300,000	0.005
TOOTHED CETACEANS AND MAN			
Sperm whale	18.8 *	74,418	0.025
Killer whale	13.3	1,091	1.22
Pilot whale	5.9	2,340	0.25
Beluga	5.1	962	0.53
Bottlenose porpoise	3.5	286	1.22
Narwhal	3.0	182	1.66
Man	3.0	171	1.74
Woman	2.7	136	2.02
Whiteside porpoise	2.5	196	1.28
Amazon porpoise	1.7	132	1.28
Harbor porpoise	1.3	165	1.29

* Two other sperm whale brains of record size have been weighed, each at 20.1 pounds.

However, the table does suggest an interesting
relationship. The brains of the sperm whale and the
killer whale are larger than one might expect. Both
animals are highly social, both are adept at echo-
locating and deep diving, both have successfully conquered the seas of all the world. Is it not reasonable to
conclude that their success is linked in some way
with a large brain?

A Natural History of Marine Mammals

Some anatomists believe that it is more the *quality* than the size of the cetacean brain which points to intelligence. In fishes and reptiles, the cerebral portion of the brain is feebly developed, but in man—the reasoning beast—it is strongly developed. (The cerebrum is the large wrinkled structure which occupies most of the cranial cavity and which is correlated with higher nervous functions.) In cetaceans, the cerebrum is even more elaborately folded and has a greater surface than in man.

According to Peter Morgane, Massachusetts neurologist, "The enormous surface of the whale cortex [rind of the cerebrum] and its luxuriant and highly convoluted appearance still appear to be sound arguments for considering the cetaceans as potentially intelligent and highly developed fellow beings" (in McIntyre, ed., *Mind in the Waters*).

In the brains of man and other newly evolved mammals, the part known as the neocortex, or new brain, is well developed. This is the part which, in man's brain at least, is continuously busy forming associations and sizing up the environment. If one ranks the brains of certain mammals according to their richness in neocortical tissue, one finds that the saddleback porpoise appears to outclass man himself. The percentage of neocortical tissue is: porpoise 97.8; man 95.9; seal 94.4; dog 84.2; kangaroo 69.2; anteater 57.2; rabbit 56.0; and hedgehog (a primitive mammal) 32.4.

But perhaps, after all, the question of intelligence in marine mammals is one that should not be raised.

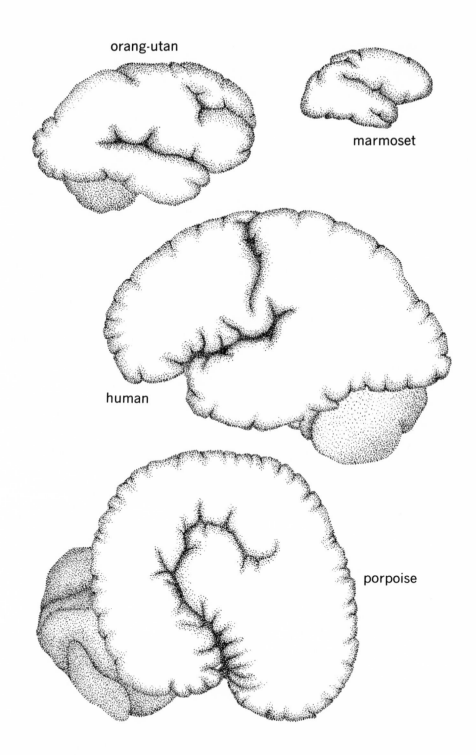

orang-utan

marmoset

human

porpoise

Figure 28 Mammalian brains

Instead of wondering whether porpoises can reason, or worry, or plan ahead as we humans do, perhaps we should simply admire their complex brains—those mysterious organs which allow them to cope with a dim, cold, watery world in which we ourselves could not long survive.

Loren Eiseley, American poet-scientist, wrote in "The Long Loneliness": "perhaps man has something to learn after all from fellow creatures [who themselves do not have] the ability to drive harpoons through living flesh."

7. REPRODUCTION

The main events in mammalian reproduction are courtship (or pairing off), physical mating, gestation of the fetus, giving birth, nursing the young, and weaning it. Reproduction among marine mammals is not unlike that among land mammals, though it does differ in three minor ways. First, marine mammals have a long gestation period. This provides for the birth of a precocious baby which will be ready for action the moment it is born. Second, the season of birth for most marine mammals is not as sharply timed as that of land mammals, the reason being that ocean temperatures are more uniform than land temperatures. Third, many marine mammals fast during their reproductive seasons. A bull Alaskan fur seal will go for 77 days without food or drink while he is on breeding duty. A female gray whale will drop in weight from 24 tons to 16 tons during her breeding fast in winter.

Figure 29   Fur seals "courting"

Reproduction

Courtship

Some marine mammals are polygynous—that is, the males have many wives. These species arrange themselves into families or harems, each dominated by a male who fathers most of the offspring in the harem. All of the walking seals (sea lions, fur seals, and walrus) are polygynous, as are two of the crawling seals—gray seal and elephant seal. At least two of the cetaceans—sperm whale and killer whale—are known to be polygynous. The bull sperm whale defends his right to guard about fifteen females in a vaguely bounded, ever-changing territory.

Among polygynous animals in general, the male is larger and stronger than the female. He has to fight; she does not. The average adult Alaskan fur seal male weighs 430 pounds as against 96 pounds for the female. A large bull sperm whale may reach 60 tons, a large female only 16 tons.

A scientist was once studying the behavior of California sea lions in captivity. There were two adult males in the group, one of which barked continuously, *"ounh! ounh! ounh!"* The other was silent. When the barker was removed to another pen, the silent one began to sound off. He now realized that *he* was free to be the aggressor, or dominant animal, in the family.

It is supposed that among all marine mammals, whether social or not, some fighting—or at least bluffing—goes on between males as a prelude to mating.

Toothed cetaceans carry body scars which, from their pattern, are made by the raking slashes of their companions' teeth. The male narwhal has a fantastic tusk —a spiral tooth which reaches a length of 9 feet and a weight of 18 pounds. Once a tusk was found jammed inside the broken shaft of another one, as though two males had rammed head-on.

Mating

The sea otter, pilot whale, killer whale, and narwhal will mate in any month of the year, though most commonly at a time which assures that the young will be born in spring or summer when food for the nursing mother will be most plentiful. In the great whales which breed in the tropics in winter and migrate to polar feeding pastures in summer, mating is sharply seasonal.

All marine mammals except the territorial seals mate in the water. The territorial seals ordinarily mate on land or on floating ice where the males can patrol their territories, though they occasionally mate in shallow water.

Sea otters mate dog-fashion, with much growling, tumbling, and biting. It is common to see a female otter with a bloody or scarred snout where some male has seized and worried her. Seals also mate dog-fashion, though the bulky gray seals and elephant seals

Figure 30   Fur seals mating

lie on their sides during the act. The mating posture of sirenians is unknown; observations of captive manatees (which may have been playing rather than mating) suggest that it is like that of cetaceans. Cetaceans mate belly-to-belly while swimming or while hanging vertically for a few seconds in the water. The humpback whale gives gigantic "love pats" to its mate with its flippers.

In some species another mating takes place soon after the female has given birth. Births are almost always single among marine mammals and the uterus has two distinct branches, so that while one branch is repairing itself after delivery the other is receptive.

So far as is known, no marine mammal goes through a change of life or menopause. In some species whose reproduction has been thoroughly studied—fur seal, sperm whale, fin whale, and blue whale—the pregnancy rate in the oldest females falls off a little.

During the long course of evolution, the bloodlines of the marine mammals and those of the land mammals moved so far apart that no marine mammal can now breed with any land mammal. However, a nearly marine mammal, the polar bear, will breed in zoos with the grizzly bear. The union produces fertile young which share body features of both parents.

Gestation

The gestation period, or time in the uterus, is well known for species such as the northern fur seal and elephant seal, which are easily observed. A scientist once built an observation tower at the edge of a fur seal rookery. He spent many days during the breeding season watching marked individuals and preparing a calendar of vital events such as mating, giving birth, nursing, and weaning. (Toward the end of summer, he had become very tired of seals.)

Gestation periods are, approximately: for the sea otter, 12 to 13 months; for the seals, 9 to 12 months; for the sirenians, unknown (1 year?); for porpoises, 8 months; and for whales, 10 to 16 months.

In all seals, the embryo remains inactive—little more than a pearly speck—during its early life. After a quiet period of several months it again begins to grow. The period of quiet, called delayed implantation, postpones the birth of the pup until the following spring or summer. The adults are thus able, when they congregate on land or ice, to give birth and to mate in one continuous breeding season. In cetaceans, growth of the embryo is never delayed, though it may proceed slowly for some weeks, then speed up explosively near the end of gestation. During the last two months of its fetal life, the blue whale grows seventy-five pounds a day.

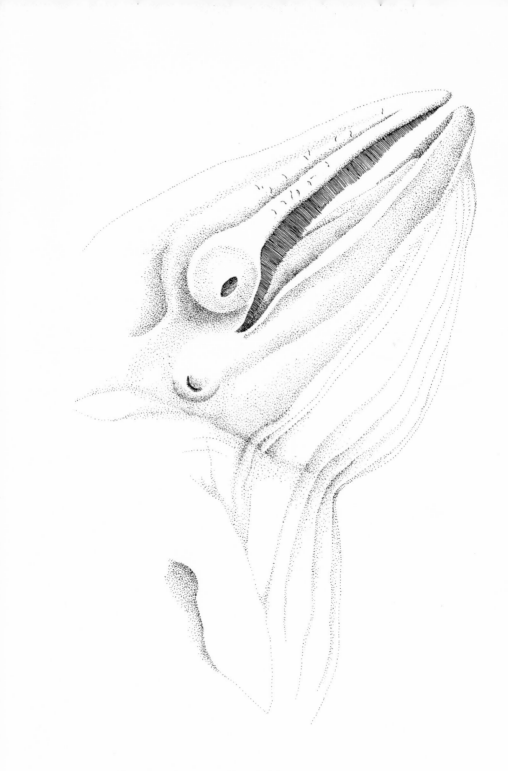

Figure 31   Fetal blue whale

Figure 32   Birth of a bottlenose porpoise

Birth

All species of seals are born on land; sirenians and cetaceans in water. No one has ever reported watching a sea otter being born. To judge from the positions of the fetuses, at least half of which lie head "aft" in the womb, at least half of the pups are born headfirst. If so, they are probably born on land like most mammals. Any marine mammal born headfirst under water might suffocate.

A Soviet scientist traveling on a research vessel had a rare opportunity to see a sperm whale birth. He saw, in a group of about forty whales, a grown female treading water with one-quarter of her body rising from the sea. As he approached, he observed beside her a 12-foot calf, still attached by the umbilical cord. The calf blew softly at intervals of one-half to one minute. Alongside the pair were two other female "aunties" who stayed completely under water and supported the calf. The calf's tail was still limp and partly curled. Evidently the little fellow had not yet stretched its muscles after a year's confinement in its mother's body.

Twins among marine mammals are rarely seen; probably few live to become independent. Nature has, so to speak, concentrated on producing one large and well-formed baby which will be able to survive the great change from the mother's warm body to the cold marine world.

Reproduction

The ringed seal is the only marine mammal born in a den, although many seals take shelter in rough ice or among rocks. The ringed seal pup is born in a den excavated in deep snow on top of sea ice or among slabs of ice.

Care of the Young

With the possible exception of the sea otter, young marine mammals are nourished on extremely rich milk. (The nature of sea-otter milk and the duration of nursing are unknown.) While cow's milk contains only 4 or 5 percent fat, that of seals contains about 50 percent and that of whales and porpoises 40 to 50 percent.

E. J. Slijper, whale expert at the University of Amsterdam, has calculated that a large whale may give 130 gallons of milk a day, in forty feedings of 3¼ gallons each. Of course no one has ever measured a whale's milk flow; it is estimated from the growth rate of the calf. Throughout its entire nursing period of six or seven months, the blue-whale calf grows at an average rate of 8.5 pounds an hour.

The greediest of young seals is the harp seal, which doubles its birth weight during its first five days of life. To learn the length of the nursing period of a gray seal, British scientists captured and held a three-day-old pup with its mother. The two were surprisingly tame. The female weaned her pup when it was eighteen days old.

A scientist from the University of California observed the behavior of northern fur seals for two summers. The average pup nursed for about four months, in ten to twelve nursing episodes spaced a little more than a week apart. Though a dozen meals in four months may seem like a skimpy diet, it raises the pup's weight from about 11 pounds to 28 pounds and prepares the pup for desertion by its mother in November.

Bottlenose porpoises in captivity nurse for a long time, up to sixteen months. Steller sea lion pups and walrus calves also nurse for more than a year. Toward the end of that time, the young one probably does not need the milk.

During its evolution, while the body of the marine mammal was becoming ever more sleek and streamlined, the female teats (nipples) were becoming fewer and smaller. Most modern marine mammals have only two. The walking seals and two kinds of crawling seals have four. Strangely, when the harbor porpoise is still in early fetal life and is only an inch long, it has eight teats. For a flashing moment, the fetus is a throwback to some land ancestor which bore young in litters.

The two teats of the manatee are located near the armpits. By a stretch of the imagination, they can be seen to resemble human breasts. Perhaps it was a female manatee, half rising from a tropical sea at dusk, that gave rise to the myth of the mermaid.

Reproduction

A young whale, having no lips, opens its jaws near one of the mother's teats while she lets milk into its mouth. The baby's tongue is free and muscular at the tip and makes a funnel for the milk. Sirenians also nurse under water, coming to the surface to breathe. The sea otter and all seals nurse in the open air.

Most mother animals will vigorously defend their newborn young. Mother sea otters and cetaceans show distress, by voice or behavior, when a person approaches the baby. The bond between the mother walrus and her calf is especially strong; an orphan walrus will accept a human foster parent with almost smothering affection. On the other hand, fur seals and sea lions seem quickly to lose interest in their young. A few days after giving birth, a mother seal will dash to the sea at the approach of a human, leaving her baby on the beach.

Many stories are told of the tender, even obsessive care which mother porpoises and whales give their young. Before there were laws against the practice, whalemen used to harpoon a suckling calf, knowing that its mother would stay nearby where she, too, could be killed. Often the mother would place herself between the calf and the whaleboat. She might even push the calf out of danger so forcefully as to break the harpoon line. William Scoresby, a famous Scottish whaleman in the early 1800s, told of a mother bowhead whale that was struck with six harpoons without leaving her baby.

The propeller of a British Columbia ferryboat accidentally slashed a young killer whale. The captain of the boat turned about and saw a male and a female supporting the bleeding calf. Fifteen days later, two whales supporting a third one—presumably the same group—were seen at the same place.

The kind of nurturant care giving which marine mammals often display seems to be instinctive and un-reasoning. Bottlenose porpoises in the wild will carry a dead and rotting calf for weeks. In an aquarium, Myrtle, a female porpoise, carried the dead body of a 5-foot shark on her snout for eight days. She kept bringing the corpse to the surface, as though she would have it breathe.

Rarely, a mother seal will adopt or even kidnap another's pup. George A. Bartholomew, a zoologist from the University of California, saw two mother fur seals fighting over a pup. "A pup slid down a slippery surface as soon as it was delivered," he wrote (in "Mother-Young Relations and the Maturation of Pup Behavior in the Alaska Fur Seal"), "and its fall broke the umbilical cord. Its mother, attempting to retrieve it . . . seized it by the skin on its back and started to lift. As she did so, a pregnant cow against which the pup had fallen seized one of its hind flippers in her mouth and a tug-of-war ensued." The rightful mother gained the victory after forty minutes; the pup did not seem to have suffered.

8. GROWTH AND LIFE SPAN

Among living organisms in general, growth in body size, as well as growth in population, can be expressed by an S-shaped curve (see diagram).

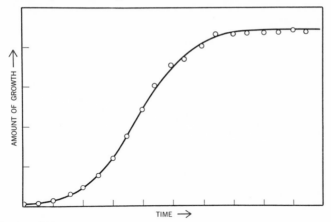

Figure 33

The curve illustrates the fact that organic growth tends to start slowly, then gradually to speed up, and then to level off when the body or the population reaches some limit imposed by its environment. Sexual maturity can be represented by a point near the steepest climb of the curve, body maturity (that is, when growth stops) by a point where the curve levels off.

Growth Indicators

Study of growth in marine mammals has been stimulated by the need to find out how quickly certain seals and whales of commercial importance reach marketable size and how fast their populations grow. Much effort has been devoted to searching for growth layers in marine mammal tissues which would be comparable to wood layers in trees.

An Australian zoologist has discovered how to tell the age of a sperm whale from its teeth. She slices a tooth lengthwise and etches it with acid. This reveals alternate layers of hard and soft ivory. Each pair of layers represents one year's growth. Similar growth layers are found in the teeth of sea otters, seals, and porpoises. They provide clues to the exact age when a female can first become pregnant, to the death rate within year-class, and to the maximum length of life.

Not only do the layers show cycles of yearly growth, they reflect good times and bad times in the life of the individual. A cross section through a fur seal tooth shows, in the youngest part of the root, ten to twelve thin layers, each representing one nursing epi-

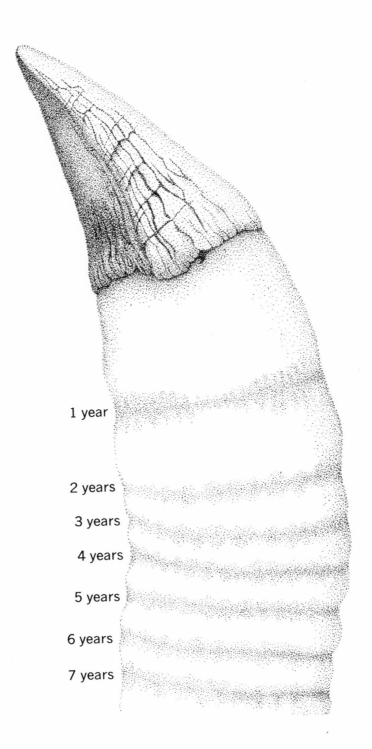

1 year

2 years

3 years

4 years

5 years

6 years

7 years

Figure 34   Growth layers in a fur seal tooth

sode. The tooth record thus confirms field observations of the behavior of the nursing pup.

The ages of baleen whales, which have no teeth, are estimated by counting growth layers in the ear plugs. The ear plug is an accumulation of horny or waxy stuff in the ear canal. Each of its layers is made up of a light streak (more fatty) laid down in summer, and a dark streak (less fatty) laid down in winter. Some scientists believe that the layering represents all that is now left of a periodic shedding of body hairs on some unknown, shaggy, ancestral "protowhale."

The layers are most clearly seen in the ears of those whales, such as the blue, fin, and humpback, which make long seasonal migrations between tropical and polar waters. The layers are usually counted on X-ray pictures taken of thin slices of ear-plug tissue, or on slices bleached by hydrogen peroxide. In both sexes of the gray whale—an intensively studied species— body maturity is reached at about age 40.

Sexual Coming of Age

Marine mammals tend to reach puberty more slowly than do land mammals of similar size. Though deer and elk will mate before their second birthday, or even before their first, the sea otter does not mate until age 2 years or older, seals at 4 to 8 years, sirenians (uncertainly) at 4 years, porpoises at 6 to 8 years, and whales at 6 to 13 years.

Not surprisingly, a marine mammal will mature later in life if it happens to grow up within a crowded, stressful population rather than within an uncrowded one. Moreover, it may be *physically* mature when still *socially* immature. Most northern fur seal males have ripe sperms in their testes when they are 4 or 5 years old but are unable to break into the social structure of the harems until later. They are "psychologically sterile." Most of the breeding, in fact, is done by bulls 9 to 11 years old. Among the gray seals of England, most of the breeding is done by bulls 12 to 18 years old, long after they have reached puberty. Male sperm whales can breed at age 13 but seldom do so until they are over 20.

Old Age

What little is known of the life spans of marine mammals has been learned in five ways: by marking animals in the wild and later catching them, by counting growth layers, by counting egg scars on ovaries, by holding individuals in captivity, and by watching distinctive individuals (such as albinos) in the wild.

On the ovaries of whales, though not of other marine mammals, the white scar which remains after the

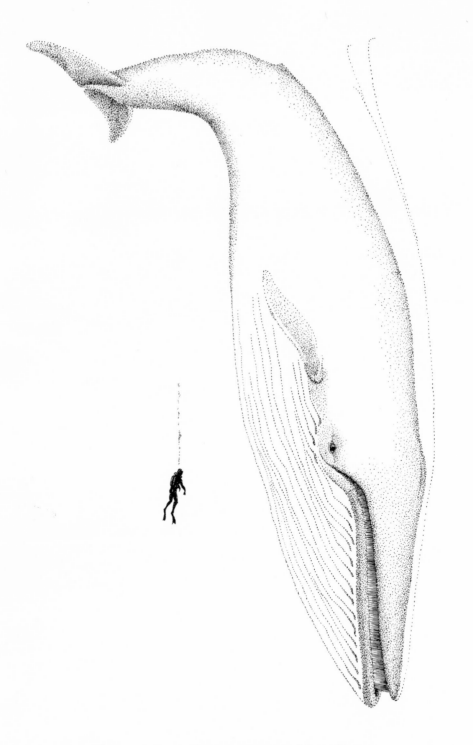

Figure 35   A 100-foot, 200-ton blue whale

shedding of each egg persists through life. Thus, if one counts the scars and knows how often the female ovulates, one can estimate her age, though not very precisely.

Pelorus Jack, a famous bottlenose porpoise, followed steamers through Pelorus Sound, New Zealand, for 32 years. A male killer whale with peculiar markings was seen along the Australian coast for more than 90 years. He was known as Old Tom. Almost certainly, though, there were several "Old Toms" of the same bloodline, separated by a generation or more.

Some age records for marine mammals are known:

Sea otter, 21 to 23 years

Walking seals, 26 (northern fur seal)

Crawling seals, 46 (gray seal) and 36 (harbor seal)

Sirenians, at least 18 (a pair of captive manatees)

Small toothed cetaceans, 30 (beluga) and 32 (bottlenose porpoise)

Large toothed cetaceans, 37 (northern bottlenose whale) and 77 (sperm whale, North Pacific)

Baleen cetaceans, 80 (fin whale, Southern Ocean)

9. MIGRATION PATTERNS

All seals, porpoises, and whales are hunters; they are constantly on the move. But the sea otter, manatee, and dugong are grazers; they feed on local organisms and remain throughout life within home ranges only a few miles wide. They are resident, or geographically sedentary, in habit.

The travels of seals and cetaceans vary in length from the short journey of a harbor seal following a change in tides to the long yearly shuttle of a gray whale between Mexico and Alaska. The harbor seal moves perhaps one thousand miles in a year; the whale, ten thousand or more.

When the annual round trip of a marine mammal between its feeding place and its breeding place covers thousands of miles and is predictably regular, it is called a migration. It resembles the migrations of swallows and geese.

In the southern hemisphere, the migrations of the rorquals are famous for their length and regularity.

Migration Patterns

(Rorqual is a whaleman's term for the blue, finback, sei, Bryde, minke, and humpback whales.) All bear their young during winter near the equator and feed during summer in icy waters to the south.

The men who hunted seals and whales long ago were dimly aware of migrations. They saw only male sperm whales in the Bering Sea in summer; both sexes near the equator in winter. They knew that harp seals would surely appear every March by the hundreds of thousands at two whelping grounds on the sea ice off Newfoundland. They saw tropical crustaceans (which they called "whale lice") clinging to the bodies of whales newly arrived in cold Antarctic feeding waters. This could only mean that the whales had traveled far and fast from warmer regions somewhere to the north. In the latter half of the nineteenth century, fragments of American bomb lances, fired into blue whales south of Newfoundland, were later found in the bodies of whales killed off Norway.

But modern sealers and whalemen are able to pinpoint the migration routes more accurately. They mark animals with numbered metal tags which they later recover, either in commercial kills or in special research hunts. In a few localities, migrating whales pass near shore where biologists can count their numbers and clock their rates of travel. Gray whales, southbound along the California coast, are counted every winter. Humpback whales, northbound between the two large islands of New Zealand, are counted in spring.

What triggers migration is not yet known. Perhaps, as with birds, it is the changing length of day from one season to the next. Migration in some marine mammals is known to be linked with changes in the sex organs, in appetite, in the thickness of body fat, and (in seals) in the shedding or molting of hair. The migrations of polar seals, all of which belong to the crawling seal group, are linked with seasonal movements of ice. In polar latitudes, a sea-ice front lies the year around at varying distances from the poles. In the North Pacific in September, the front lies north of the Bering Strait; in March, south of the Strait.

To navigate in the trackless ocean, marine mammals doubtless use all of their senses together. Their guides or seamarks are thought to be wind currents, water currents, submarine contours (the ridges and valleys of the sea floor), taste and temperature of the water, and direction of the sun and moon. Porpoises in the Mediterranean Sea are known to use the sun as a compass as they travel daily to and from their feeding waters.

The following accounts of the journeys of two outstanding migrators—gray whale and harp seal—are partly fictional.

A Gray Whale's Migration

A female gray whale, heavy with unborn calf, is feeding in the Arctic Ocean on the last day of September when instinct tells her to turn southward. Filmy new ice is forming each night over the channels where she feeds. She heads for the Bering Sea near the end of a ragged line of migrating companions. Then, gradually losing her taste for food, she enters the Pacific Ocean. She follows the coastline south, swimming 5 miles an hour and over 100 miles a day as she nears her goal. In mid-December, she crosses the shallow bar of Scammon's Lagoon, on the coast of Baja California, Mexico.

She gives birth on Christmas Day. Twelve hundred other pregnant or newly postpartum (calved) females are gathered in five lagoons of western Mexico. Nowhere else in the world does her kind breed. She will not remate for a year or two.

Inside the lagoon and in the nearby Pacific Ocean, she nurses her calf until early March, losing in the meanwhile 8 tons of body weight. Mother and calf then move slowly out to sea and northward, heading for Alaska along a course which is still unknown to man. At the end of July, after nursing her calf for seven months, she weans it. Once again feeding greedily, she enters the Arctic Ocean, while some of her companions move westward to waters off Siberia.

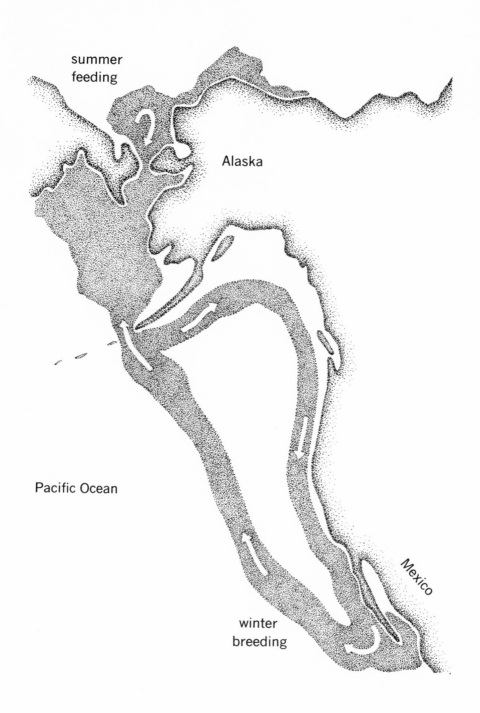

summer feeding

Alaska

Pacific Ocean

Mexico

winter breeding

Figure 36   The range of the gray whales

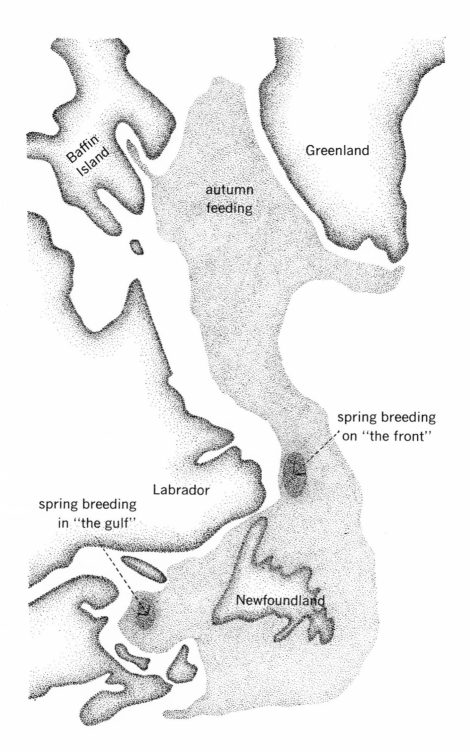

Figure 37 The range of the Northwest Atlantic harp seals

A Harp Seal's Migration

A pregnant harp seal is feeding in September above the Arctic Circle in Davis Strait, between Canada and Greenland. She is one of a million Northwest Atlantic harp seals. As the autumn sea-ice front moves slowly southward, she travels ahead of it. Feeding on capelin and cod, she grows very fat. In December she sights Newfoundland. Here the seals divide into two bands according to their memories of the places where they were born—either "The Front" or "The Gulf." The Front band migrates toward its whelping ground on the ice west of Labrador; she herself is part of the band heading for the whelping ground in the Gulf of St. Lawrence.

In mid-March, she gives birth to a woolly "whitecoat," a beautiful pup all white except for its black eyes and snout. It grows rapidly on mother's milk. By early April it has taught itself to swim and to feed on plankton crustaceans and small fish. Deserted by its mother, it joins others of its age. Mother mates again at the edge of ice in May.

During early summer, the adults and juveniles (the young ones older than pups) spend a good deal of time loafing on the ice while their hairy coats are molting. By midsummer, all are moving slowly northward into Davis Strait, and by September they are feeding again above the Circle. In their migration, some adults have traveled 5,000 miles.

Offbeat Migrations

In addition to regular migrants, there always seem to be a few marine mammals that, through accident or choice, strike out on their own. Fur seals tagged as pups on the American shore have been recovered on the Asian shore, and vice versa. An elephant seal was found dead on an Alaskan beach 2,000 miles from Mexico, the nearest breeding place of the species. A ribbon seal which could only have come from the Arctic crawled out on a beach of central California. It was ill and doubtless confused.

A killer whale once ascended the freshwater Columbia River for a distance of 110 miles to the city of Portland, Oregon. There it thrilled many thousands who had never before seen a whale. It was killed by two selfish men who embalmed it and placed it on exhibition for a fee.

Far inland from the sea, on the icy continent of Antarctica, explorers often find the mummified bodies of seals. These are leathery and worn, scoured by wind and driven snow. Some are hundreds of years old. A crabeater pup was once captured alive wandering at an elevation of 3,000 feet and 70 miles from the nearest water. The survival of nomadic pups for what must be weeks without food, and in freezing weather, illustrates the incredible vitality of marine mammals.

10. DISEASES AND OTHER HAZARDS

The Weddell seal of Antarctica, cutting holes in the sea ice through which it can breathe, uses its upper teeth as a saw. The teeth suffer wear. In many old individuals, tooth decay sets in and the animal dies of infection, or it suffocates beneath the ice, or it starves because it cannot catch fish.

But unhappy endings are the fate of all wild creatures. None dies peacefully of old age. The lives of all are ended by accident, starvation, exposure, disease, or predation. Harmful factors in the lives of animals should not necessarily be thought of as bad, for although they weaken or kill individuals they maintain the health and stability of species. They tend continually to weed out the unfit. Nature pays a premium for those Weddell seals which inherit the strongest teeth.

Over a long period of time, the total number of individuals in any population which die tends to equal those which are born. In the Alaskan fur seal herd

Figure 38   Fur seal pup; storm victim

about 360,000 pups are born each year and about 360,000 seals of all ages—from newborn to age 26 years—die each year.

The list of harmful factors in the lives of marine mammals is a long one.

Parasites and Diseases

Among the parasites known to infest marine mammals are roundworms (trichina, hookworm, and others), tapeworms, flukes, spiny-headed worms, lice, and nasal mites. Among disease organisms (or "germs") are viruses, bacteria, protozoans, and fungi. Marine mammals suffer from pneumonia, tuberculosis, cancer, stomach ulcers, epilepsy, and indeed most of the ailments with which man is distressingly familiar.

Marine mammals may even become psychotic. Bimbo, a pilot whale who lived for eight years in a public oceanarium, developed symptoms which in a human might be called manic-depressive. He was mercifully shipped out to sea and turned loose.

Some of the organisms which cause disease in marine mammals can be passed on to man or to his domestic animals such as cows and pigs. Among these organisms are the ones which cause childhood pneumonia, contagious abortion, and the painful ailment known as trichinosis. Others will doubtless be discovered.

Diseases and Other Hazards

Approaching the status of parasites are "fellow travelers" which attach to the bodies of seals and whales without doing material harm. These include diatoms, algae, protozoans, barnacles, tiny crablike crustaceans, and whalesuckers (fish).

Found each year on the California coast are the bodies of small sea lion pups—the victims of natural abortion. Among the suspected causes are a bacterium (*Leptospira*), the San Miguel sea lion virus, and chemical poisons.

Contaminants

Many poisons, including insect sprays, weed killers, lead from automobile exhausts, and manufacturing wastes such as cadmium, mercury, and arsenic, find their way into the sea. Here they enter the bodies of primary producers (mainly unicellular plants on the bottom rung of the food ladder). Because many of the poisons are resistant to natural decay, they tend to accumulate in the bodies of marine mammals—the organisms highest on the ladder.

Rarely does a contaminant kill outright. More often it weakens the mammal, making it more likely to die during bad weather or less able to escape the rush of a shark or killer whale. The most serious effect of a contaminant is damage to the animal's sex organs. The effect can most clearly be seen when poisons measured in the tissues can be linked with field observations of reduced birthrate.

Collectors for a Florida aquarium salvaged a rare 570-pound pygmy sperm whale from the beach. It died a week later. An autopsy showed that it had swallowed a large plastic bag of the kind that fishermen often carry on their boats. Many zoo seals and porpoises die from the effects of copper pennies, broken bottles, beach balls, and other objects tossed into their pools by thoughtless visitors.

Predators

Mention was made in Chapter 4 of the killer whale, leopard seal, sea lion, and rogue walrus which attack and devour other marine mammals. Even more important as enemies of the marine mammals are the great white shark and tiger shark of warm seas and the Greenland shark of colder seas, all of which have earned the name "man-eater." A dead sea otter that washed ashore on a California beach was clearly the victim of a shark, for one of the teeth of the man-eater was still embedded in its fur.

In Alaska, polar bears habitually stalk and kill seals and walruses, while the little Arctic fox will now and then surprise a ringed seal pup at its whelping place on the ice.

Figure 39 *Polar bear*

It is from the youngest individuals of a population that predators take their heaviest toll. As the little seal or porpoise grows older, stronger, and more agile, and as it learns by watching its elders, its chances for survival increase. It learns evasive swimming and diving and ways to strike defensive blows with its body.

Once, when a catcher-boat fired a harpoon into a sperm whale off Japan, ten of its companions quickly arranged themselves into a daisy-petal pattern with their heads pointing toward a common center. In this defensive pattern, their powerful tails were in a position to repel the strange "predator" which seemed about to attack them.

Accidents

Sometimes toothed whales and porpoises will rush into shallow water, run aground on the beach, and die. As many as two hundred may strand themselves in what have been called "mass suicides." Among baleen whales, stranding is rare.

One cause of stranding may be that the echolocation system fails when an animal swims too close to a gently sloping beach. Another cause may be injuries from parasitic worms which crawl into the nasal passages, inner ears, and even brain tissues. Parasites may cause the host animal to become dizzy and then to be cast ashore by waves and currents.

Figure 40   Stranded Bryde whale

A Natural History of Marine Mammals

In 1957 a party of British explorers traveling on the sea ice off Antarctica came upon several small pools in the ice through which minke, killer, and beaked whales were rising to breathe. The whales had been trapped by the sudden freezing of a shallow harbor entrance. The men formed a Pat-the-Whale Club for those who managed to touch a whale's snout as it rose.

Icing in, as this sort of accident is called, is not uncommon in polar regions. More than a thousand narwhals were once trapped near Greenland, where they were subsequently killed by Eskimos.

In the early 1960s, men fishing for tuna in the tropical Pacific Ocean began to use a method they called "setting on porpoise." They would spread a huge net around a school of porpoises, knowing from experience that tuna habitually swim beneath such schools. As the men closed the net, hundreds of porpoises suffocated. Many sensitive Americans did not like to hear the term accident used to describe what was, in a sense, deliberate killing. When, in 1972, the death rate rose to over 300,000 porpoises a year, the United States Government passed a law forcing the fishermen to search for methods of sparing the mammals.

11. HOW MARINE MAMMALS ARE STUDIED

The world ocean is a new frontier of science. Zoologists are inventing new tools and operations which are shedding light on the mysterious lives of the sea otter, seals, sirenians, and cetaceans. Often these men and women study animals living freely in the wild, though more often they study tame animals in captivity.

In the Wild

For the conservation of any animal species, one must know the size of its population, or at least know whether the population is rising, falling, or holding its own. For this purpose, counts of marine mammals are made from aircraft, ships, and observation towers on land.

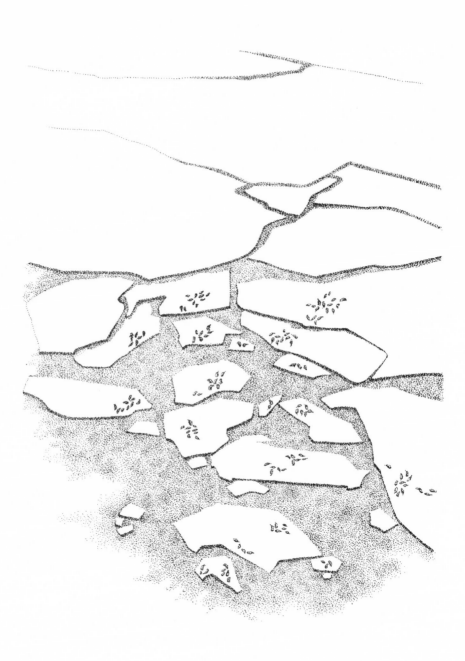

Figure 41　Harp seals viewed from the air

How Marine Mammals Are Studied

One zoologist took an aerial photograph showing 1,071 sea otters in a single huge "raft." Another circled in a helicopter above the Sixty-Mile Bank off the coast of California. He counted more than 2,000 porpoises of 4 species and 3 gray whales and saw vast numbers of sea birds. The mammals and the birds were feeding on a school of small fishes which continually broke the surface of the sea.

One task in any population study is to map the boundaries of the home range of the species. This is best done by marking sample individuals, releasing them, and following their movements by sight or by instrument. A package fastened to the animal's body which broadcasts its position by radiotelemetry is one such instrument. The package is designed to release itself from the body after some weeks and thus spare its host further discomfort. All sorts of metal and plastic tags, collars, and girdles have been fastened to marine mammals. Paints, hair bleaches, laser brands, and freeze brands have also been used. In freeze branding, a copper tool is chilled by "dry ice" (solid carbon dioxide) and is pressed to the animal's skin for a few seconds. It kills the pigment cells without harming the surrounding cells, leaving a white symbol that remains throughout life.

Of course it is necessary to capture and hold an animal before instruments can be attached or marks be applied. Seals are temporarily drugged by means of a hypodermic syringe fired into the body. They recover

Figure 42   Preparing to tag a newborn harbor seal

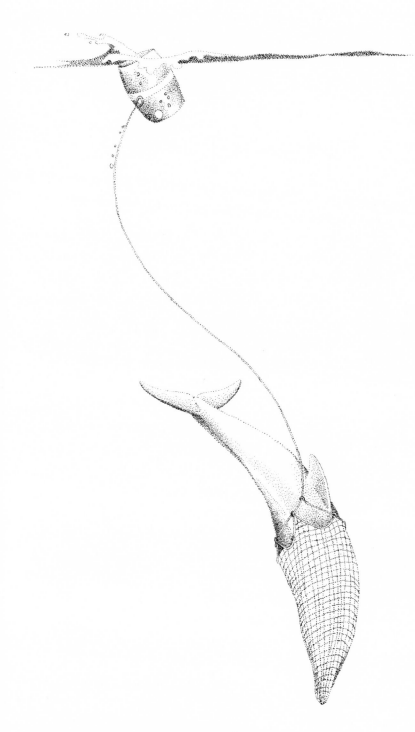

Figure 43   Live-netting a porpoise

to find themselves carrying a strange new burden. Nets are used to capture porpoises.

Tamed and in Captivity

In 1971, a team of scientists captured a baby gray whale in a Mexican lagoon. They named her Gigi and took her to an oceanarium in California where she was weaned and held under observation. When they finally released her in the Pacific Ocean a year later, she had become famous as the largest whale ever to be tamed and studied for more than a few days. She became the more or less willing subject of many scientifically valuable studies.

A harmless radioactive tracer was injected into her bloodstream. After a few minutes, during which time the tracer circulated through her system, samples of blood were drawn and analyzed. Her body contained 1.24 ounces of blood per pound of body weight, or about the same ratio as in a grown man.

Her 5-ton body was lifted on a canvas stretcher to which had been fastened a ballistocardiograph recorder. The instrument measured the slight "bowl of jelly" trembling of her body at each beat of her heart. Indirectly, it measured her blood flow. Her heart was pumping 81 gallons, or about 2 barrels, a minute.

A few drops of her blood were treated in a laboratory to reveal their microscopic chromosomes, or units of heredity. These were photographed and mounted as a chromosome map. The study was part of a larger one designed to show the family relationships of the cetaceans. Chromosomes are conservative parts of any living organism; they tend to evolve more slowly than do other body structures.

Scientists came from all over the world to study Gigi. At the same time, other scientists were studying Skana, a beautiful 20-foot female killer whale in Vancouver Public Aquarium. Gigi was a baleen whale; Skana was a toothed whale.

The amount of food eaten daily by a large whale in the wild cannot be directly measured but can be estimated through a series of calculations which involve (1) the amounts of food eaten by various kinds of smaller cetaceans in captivity, (2) the body weights and heart weights of these smaller animals, and (3) the body weight and heart weight of the whale. The calculation depends on the fact that both heart weight and feeding rate are expressions of metabolic rate, or "speed of living."

A blue whale was once weighed piecemeal by Norwegian whalemen; it tipped the scales at 196 tons. Alive, it may have eaten 4 to 8 tons of plankton a day.

A scientist tested the ability of a California sea lion to tell the size of objects under water. On buzzer command, the tame animal would swim toward two targets, both white and circular but of different sizes. If the animal chose the larger target, it got a fish reward. Gradually the experimenter substituted targets

Figure 44   Sea lion taking a visual test

which were more and more nearly alike in size. He found that the animal could identify a target which was less than 1 percent larger than the other.

People often ask whether porpoises sleep. Some years ago, John C. Lilly, an American student of porpoise behavior, stationed two watchmen, one on the right side and one on the left side of a porpoise resting in a narrow tub of water. In 24 hours, the animal closed both eyes for less than 5 minutes and closed each eye separately for 3 or 4 hours. It seemed to be sleeping on those occasions—but was it? (Reported by Gregory Bateson, in McIntyre, ed., *Mind in the Waters.*)

Other researchers gave a stricter test, this time to tame gray seals. They studied the electrical waves in the brain, the eye movements beneath closed lids, and the heart rates. Changes in these vital signs were telemetered to a recording instrument near the animals' pool. Judged by their nervous reactions, the seals did indeed sleep for as long as 4 hours at a time. Sometimes they rested for many minutes at the bottom of the pool, though at such times the instrument showed that they were not really sleeping.

Scientists are carrying on many other kinds of research on marine mammals. They are asking how and when the beasts of the sea first entered the aquatic world and how they have accommodated to living there. If there is any one general thrust of research, it is toward learning about the lives of the mammals in their wild, natural habitat. Some of the finest research data are being obtained by watching, from special submarines, underwater tanks, or diving helmets, the behavior of free subjects. Watching unrestrained animals is the most humane method and the one most likely to return evidence of the truth.

12. EXTINCTION OR SURVIVAL?

The Steller sea cow was exterminated by hunters in 1768. During the 1940s, the last of the Caribbean monk seals, Japanese sea lions, and Korean gray whales were killed. Today, certain stocks of whales are gravely threatened. Worldwide, the fin whales are down to 22 percent of their original numbers, the humpback whale to 14 percent, and the blue whales to 6 percent.

But there are encouraging signs. Many animal-welfare groups and humane societies have adopted the whale as a symbol of a natural good—something beautiful and wonderful that mankind is in danger of losing. The danger is posed by overhunting and by fouling of the whale's environment through man's wastes and poisons. Governments, too, are showing concern for the whales. The United States and Canada brought an end to all whaling along their shores in 1971 and 1972. Congress, in 1972, passed the Marine Mammal Protection Act, which is aimed at safeguarding the welfare of wild populations and, moreover,

Figure 45   The last sea cow

Extinction or Survival?

promoting humane methods of killing, as well as of capturing and holding them.

The management and protection of marine mammal stocks will call for economic trade-offs. Commercial fishermen in the Bering Sea are now taking so many fish that the Alaskan fur seal herd has stopped growing in numbers. Mother seals, to provide milk for their pups on the beach, must catch and eat fish during the summer. Each mother needs 500 to 600 pounds of food during the four-month nursing period. But in competition with man, the mother gets fewer fish, she produces less milk, and at the end of summer the average pup is smaller than it used to be before the Bering Sea was overfished. The smaller pup is more likely to die during its first winter at sea. A trade-off must be made between the people who want profits from fish and those who want profits from sealskin coats.

Similar competition, affecting harp seals, is developing off the coast of Canada. The 1 million seals of the Newfoundland herd eat annually about 1.5 million tons of crustaceans and fish—especially polar cod and capelin. Where lie the boundaries between the needs of seals and the needs of men?

The word conservation is often used to describe efforts to save wild animals from extinction or to use them wisely for man's welfare. Charles S. Elton, pioneer ecologist of Oxford University, believes that the central good of conservation is *variety* (*The Ecology of Invasions by Animals and Plants*). There are, he says, three reasons for saving variety:

Because it helps to maintain stability—that is, environmental resistance to invading "weed" species and resistance to violent fluctuations in the number of native species.

Because it gives mankind opportunity for richer experience. (For example, porpoises, through their pure animal awareness and completeness, expand and enrich our imaginative lives.)

Because it is a natural or "right" sort of relation between people and other living things.

The conservation of marine mammals, then, becomes an effort to preserve the variety of sea otters, seals, sirenians, and cetaceans in a world daily being modified by man.

Figure 46   Sea otter mother and pup

APPENDIXES

BIBLIOGRAPHY

INDEX

~∾ ∾~

APPENDIX I:
WHERE TO SEE
MARINE MAMMALS

One can see wild sea otters in the kelp along the central California coast at all times of the year. Point Lobos State Park and other headlands from Monterey south to Morro Bay are good viewing places.

The great Alaskan fur seal herd is at its best in July and August. Tourist planes fly weekly or oftener in summer from Anchorage to St. Paul Island. Sea lions, absent from North Atlantic waters, can be seen at Sea Lion Rocks near Florence, Oregon, and at many places along the California coast, including San Francisco (Seal Rocks), Monterey, and Point Lobos. Tourist boats run from Santa Barbara to the Channel Islands, rich in bird life and sea lions.

Harbor seals are uncommon south of Alaska and shy everywhere. With binoculars, one may spot them on the Olympic coast and in Grays Harbor, Washington; at the north end of San Francisco Bay; and at Boothbay Harbor, Maine. They do not breed south of Maine on the Atlantic coast. In United States waters, elephant seals live almost entirely on sanctuary islands such as Año Nuevo, the Farallons, and San Miguel, all off California; however, they are now beginning to appear in small numbers on the mainland north of Santa Cruz, California, in San Mateo County Park.

Some of the best photographs of manatees have been taken underwater in clear, spring-fed headwaters of the Crystal River, 65 miles north of Tampa, Florida. Visitors (but not swimmers or divers) are welcome at the Blue Springs Park manatee preserve 30 miles north of Orlando, Florida. From a boat or from the shore, though, one gets a disappointing view of any sirenian —little more than a pair of black, flaring nostrils in a gray, rubbery head.

One is unlikely to see porpoises unless one travels on the ocean. Some species like to play in the bow waves of small vessels. Killer whales are often seen in hunting packs of about ten in Puget Sound, Washington, though not predictably so.

To be sure of seeing a baleen whale, one should visit Cabrillo National Monument, San Diego, California, from mid-December to mid-February. Here, from a "whale overlook," one can see the 10-foot spouts of gray whales migrating southward, singly or in small groups, just beyond the kelp beds. In December, one may see them from Florence and Port Orford, Oregon; and from Crescent City, Patrick Point, and Trinidad Head, California.

Millions of Americans unable to travel to the wild environments of the marine mammals are learning

Appendix I

about harbor seals, California sea lions, bottlenose porpoises, and other commonly displayed species by observing them in oceanariums. The location of oceanariums, some of which are far inland, can be learned from local tourist guides, or one can consult, in libraries, the latest edition of a directory entitled *Zoos and Aquariums in the Americas* published by the American Association of Zoological Parks and Aquariums, Oglebay Park, Wheeling, West Virginia.

APPENDIX II:
CLASSIFICATION
OF MARINE MAMMALS

All marine mammals belong to the class Mammalia and are further classified by orders, families, genera, and species. The scientific name of an organism usually consists of two terms: one for the genus followed by one for the species. For example, man is *Homo sapiens*. Generic and specific names are customarily set in italic type; all other categorical names, as well as common or vernacular names, in roman type.

Order	Family	Scientific Name	Common Name
		GROUP 1. SEA OTTERS	
Carnivora	Mustelidae	*Enhydra lutris*	sea otter
		GROUP 2. WALKING SEALS	
Carnivora	Otariidae	*Otaria flavescens*	South American sea lion
		Phocarctos hookeri	New Zealand sea lion
		Zalophus californianus	California sea lion
		Neophoca cinerea	Australian sea lion
		Eumetopias jubatus	Steller sea lion
		Callorhinus ursinus	northern fur seal

Order	Family	Scientific Name	Common Name

Order	Family	Scientific Name	Common Name
GROUP 2. WALKING SEALS (*continued*)			
		Arctocephalus townsendi	Guadalupe fur seal *
	Odobenidae	*Odobenus rosmarus*	walrus
GROUP 3. CRAWLING SEALS			
Carnivora	Phocidae	*Phoca vitulina*	harbor seal
		Phoca hispida	ringed seal
		Phoca sibirica	Baikal seal
		Phoca caspica	Caspian seal
		Phoca groenlandica	harp seal
		Phoca fasciata	ribbon seal
		Halichoerus grypus	gray seal
		Erignathus barbatus	bearded seal
		Cystophora cristata	hooded seal
		Monachus monachus	Mediterranean monk seal
		Monachus schauinslandi	Hawaiian monk seal
		Lobodon carcinophagus	crabeater seal
		Ommatophoca rossi	Ross seal
		Hydrurga leptonyx	leopard seal
		Leptonychotes weddelli	Weddell seal
		Mirounga leonina	southern elephant seal
		Mirounga angustirostris	northern elephant seal
GROUP 4. SIRENIANS			
Sirenia	Dugongidae	*Dugong dugon*	dugong
	Trichechidae	*Trichechus manatus*	Caribbean manatee
		Trichechus senegalensis	West African manatee
		Trichechus inunguis	Amazon manatee
GROUP 5. TOOTHED CETACEANS			
Cetacea, suborder Odontoceti	Platanistidae	*Platanista gangetica*	susu or India river porpoise

* This species breeds on Guadalupe Island, Mexico. Seven other species, not listed here, breed on the equator or south of it.

Order	Family	Scientific Name	Common Name

Order	Family	Scientific Name	Common Name
		Inia geoffrensis	boutu or Amazon porpoise
		Lipotes vexillifer	Chinese lake porpoise or white flag porpoise
		Pontoporia blainvillei	franciscana or La Plata porpoise
	Delphinidae	*Delphinus delphis*	saddleback porpoise
		Steno bredanensis	rough-tooth porpoise
		Sousa chinensis	Asiatic sousa
		Sousa teuszi	African sousa
		Sotalia fluviatilis	tucuxi or tookashee
		Tursiops truncatus	bottlenose porpoise
		Stenella longirostris	spinner porpoise
		Stenella (species?)	spotted porpoise *
		Stenella coeruleoalba	blue-white porpoise
		Lagenodelphis hosei	Fraser porpoise
		Lagenorhynchus albirostris	whitebeak porpoise
		Lagenorhynchus acutus	Atlantic whiteside porpoise
		Lagenorhynchus obliquidens **	Pacific white-side porpoise
		Cephalorhynchus commersoni ***	Commerson porpoise

* There are probably two or more species of spotted porpoise; their classification is still uncertain.

** Three other species of *Lagenorhynchus* from the Southern Ocean have been described.

*** This and three other species of *Cephalorhynchus* live only in the Southern Ocean.

Order	Family	Scientific Name	Common Name

GROUP 5. TOOTHED CETACEANS (*continued*)

	Platanis-tidae	*Lissodelphis borealis*	northern right-whale porpoise
		Lissodelphis peroni	southern right-whale porpoise
		Grampus griseus	gray grampus
		Peponocephala electra	melon-head whale
		Feresa attenuata	pygmy killer whale
		Pseudorca crassidens	false killer whale
		Globicephala melaena	longfin pilot whale
		Globicephala macro-rhynchus	shortfin pilot whale
		Orcinus orca	killer whale or orca
		Orcaella brevirostris	Irawaddy porpoise
		Phocoena phocoena °	harbor porpoise
		Neophocaena phocaenoides	finless porpoise
		Phocoenoides dalli	Dall porpoise
	Monodon-tidae	*Monodon monoceros*	narwhal
		Delphinapterus leucas	white whale or beluga
	Physeteridae	*Physeter catodon*	sperm whale
		Kogia breviceps	pygmy sperm whale
		Kogia simus	dwarf sperm whale
	Ziphiidae	*Ziphius cavirostris*	goosebeak whale
		Berardius arnouxi	Arnoux beaked whale
		Berardius bairdi	Baird beaked whale
		Tasmacetus shepherdi	Tasman beaked whale

° Three other species of *Phocoena*, all resembling the harbor porpoise, have been described.

Order	Family	Scientific Name	Common Name

GROUP 5. TOOTHED CETACEANS (*continued*)

Order	Family	Scientific Name	Common Name
		Hyperoodon ampullatus	northern bottle-nose whale
		Hyperoodon planifrons	southern bottle-nose whale
		Mesoplodon stejnegeri *	Stejneger beaked whale

GROUP 6. BALEEN CETACEANS

Order	Family	Scientific Name	Common Name
Cetacea, suborder Mysticeti	Eschrich-tiidae	*Eschrictius robustus*	gray whale
	Balaeno-pteridae	*Balaenoptera acutorostrata*	minke whale or little piked whale
		Balaenoptera borealis	sei whale
		Balaenoptera edeni	Bryde whale
		Balaenoptera physalus	fin whale or finback whale
		Balaenoptera musculus	blue whale
		Megaptera novaeangliae	humpback whale
	Balaenidae	*Balaena glacialis*	right whale or black right whale
		Balaena mysticetus	bowhead or Greenland right whale
		Caperea marginata	pygmy right whale

* Eleven other species of *Mesoplodon*, including one in a new genus "*Indopacetus*," have been described.

≈≈

BIBLIOGRAPHY

Marine mammals are of worldwide interest. This list includes books and articles published in other countries as well as in the United States. In addition to the annotated entries, sources of quotations in the text are given.

Andersen, Harald T., ed. *The Biology of Marine Mammals.* New York: Academic Press, 1969.
Technical; high-quality articles though incomplete coverage of the field.

Audubon [Magazine], vol. 77, no. 1 (January 1975).
Special issue on cetaceans; many colored illustrations.

Bartholomew, George A. "Mother-Young Relations and the Maturation of Pup Behaviour in the Alaska Fur Seal," *Animal Behaviour,* vol. 7, no. 3–4 (1959): 165–166.

Bertram, G. C. L., and Bertram, C. Kate. "The Modern Sirenia: Their Distribution and Status," *Biological Journal of the Linnaean Society,* vol. 5, no. 4 (1973): 297–338.

Bibliography

The only modern comprehensive report on dugongs and manatees.

Caldwell, David K., and Caldwell, Melba C. *The World of the Bottlenosed Dolphin.* Philadelphia: Lippincott, 1972.
The authors personally studied the biology of porpoises in oceanariums and in the wild.

Conly, Robert Leslie. "Porpoises: Our Friends in the Sea," *National Geographic Magazine,* vol. 130, no. 3 (September 1966): 396–425.
Early efforts to understand porpoise "speech" and echo-location; richly illustrated.

Daugherty, Anita E. *Marine Mammals of California.* Sacramento: California Department of Fish and Game, 1972. Paperback.
Broad coverage; sketches; keys to species.

Eiseley, Loren. "The Long Loneliness. Man and the Porpoise: Two Solitary Destinies," *American Scholar,* Winter 1960–61, p. 63.

Elton, Charles S. *The Ecology of Invasions by Animals and Plants.* London: Chapman and Hall, 1958, chapters 8 and 9.

Harrison, Richard J., ed. *Functional Anatomy of Marine Mammals.* 2 vols. New York and London: Academic Press, 1972–1974.
This technical work, edited by a British physiologist, contains bibliographies which serve as a guide to the world's literature on marine mammal biology.

Harrison, Richard J., and King, Judith E. *Marine Mammals.* London: Hutchinson, 1965; paperback reprint 1973.
Technical; incomplete coverage; good bibliography.

Bibliography

Hartman, Daniel S. "Florida's Manatees, Mermaids in Peril," *National Geographic Magazine,* vol. 136, no. 3 (September 1969): 342–353.
Includes color photographs taken under water.

Husar, Sandra L. "The Dugong: Endangered Siren of the South Seas," *National Parks and Conservation Magazine,* vol. 49, no. 2 (February 1975): 15–18. The author is a specialist on sirenians for the United States Fish and Wildlife Service.

Kenyon, Karl W. *The Sea Otter in the Eastern Pacific Ocean.* Fish and Wildlife Service, North American Fauna no. 68 (1969). Paperback.
Monograph; technical but readable.

King, Judith E. *Seals of the World.* London: British Museum (Natural History), 1964. Paperback.
Excellent coverage, though some scientific names are out of date. (Crabeater seal quote, p. 70.)

Lilly, John C. *The Mind of the Dolphin: A Nonhuman Intelligence.* Garden City, N.Y.: Doubleday, 1967.
Describes attempts to communicate with porpoises.

McIntyre, Joan, ed. *Mind in the Waters.* New York: Charles Scribner's Sons; San Francisco: Sierra Club. 1974. Also in paperback.
Twenty-four authors, in language ranging from poetical to scientific, explain the importance of cetaceans to man; a beautiful and thoughtful book. Illustrated. The following articles are quoted in the present book:

Bateson, Gregory. "Observations of a Cetacean Community," pp. 157–158.

Bibliography

Bunnell, Sterling. "The Evolution of Cetacean Intelligence," p. 58.

Morgane, Peter. "The Whale Brain: The Anatomical Basis of Intelligence," p. 89.

Mackintosh, N. A. *The Stocks of Whales.* London: Fishing News (Books), 1965.
Historical account of world whale management by a man who was involved in it from 1924 to 1973.

McNulty, Faith. *The Great Whales.* Garden City, N.Y.: Doubleday, 1975.
A small book written with literary skill by a frequent contributor to *The New Yorker.*

Mansfield, Arthur W. *Seals of Arctic and Eastern Canada.* Ottawa: Fisheries Research Board of Canada, 1967. Paperback.
Diagnostic sketches; distribution maps.

Matthews, Leonard Harrison, ed. *The Whale.* London: Allen and Unwin; New York: Crown, Crescent Books.
A richly illustrated popular account of the cetaceans of the world.

Miller, Tom. *The World of the California Gray Whale.* Santa Ana, Calif.: Baja Trail Publications, 1975. Paperback.
A pocket-size encyclopedia of information on marine mammals of the Pacific United States.

Mörzer Bruyns, W. F. J. *Field Guide of Whales and Dolphins.* Amsterdam: Uitgeverij Tor, 1971.
Perhaps the best modern guide to species of cetaceans of the world; detailed facts and figures. Color plates, charts, and graphs.

Bibliography

Norris, Kenneth S. *The Porpoise Watcher*. New York: W. W. Norton, 1974.
Fascinating personal account of methods for studying cetaceans. The author is an American authority on cetacean behavior.

Norris, Kenneth S., ed. *Whales, Dolphins, and Porpoises: Proceedings of the 1st International Symposium on Cetacean Research*. Berkeley: University of California Press, 1966.
Technical.

Orr, Robert T. *Marine Mammals of California*. California Natural History Guides no. 29. Berkeley: University of California Press, 1972. Paperback.
A pocket guide.

Pike, Gordon C., and MacAskie, I. Brian. *Marine Mammals of British Columbia*. Fisheries Research Board of Canada, Bulletin 171 (1969). Paperback.
Specimen records, whaling data, species accounts, and photographs.

Ponting, Herbert George. *Scott's Last Voyage, through the Antarctic Camera of Herbert Ponting*. Ed. Ann Savours. New York: Praeger, 1975, p. 61.

Pryor, Karen W. "Behavior and Learning in Porpoises and Whales," *Naturwissenschaften*, Jahrg. 60, Heft 9 (1973): 417.

————. *Lads Before the Wind: Adventures in Porpoise Training*. New York: Harper & Row, 1975.
Introduction by Konrad Lorentz. Lively story of eight years of "behavior-shaping" of porpoises for Hawaii's Sea Life Park.

Rice, Charles E., principal ed. *The Behavior and*

Bibliography

Physiology of Pinnipeds. New York: Appleton-Century-Crofts, 1968.
Technical.

Rice, Dale W., and Scheffer, Victor B. *A List of the Marine Mammals of the World.* Bureau of Commercial Fisheries Special Scientific Report—Fisheries, no. 579 (1968).
The only distributional checklist in English giving scientific and vernacular names. A revision by Dale W. Rice is scheduled for publication in 1976.

Rice, Dale W., and Wolman, Allen A. *The Life History and Ecology of the Gray Whale* (Eschrichtius robustus). American Society of Mammalogists, Special Publication no. 3 (1971).
Technical.

Ridgway, Sam H., ed. *Mammals of the Sea: Biology and Medicine.* Springfield, Ill.: Charles C. Thomas, 1972.
Technical.

Scheffer, Victor B. *The Year of the Seal.* New York: Charles Scribner's Sons, 1970. Also in paperback.
One year in the life of a northern fur seal; fiction based on fact.

———. *The Year of the Whale.* New York: Charles Scribner's Sons, 1969. Also in paperback.
One year in the life of a sperm whale; fiction based on fact.

Schevill, William E., ed. *The Whale Problem: A Status Report.* Cambridge: Harvard University Press, 1974.
Technical report of an international conference on the biology of whales held in 1971.

Bibliography

Scoresby, William, Jr. *An Account of the Arctic Regions, with a History and Description of the Northern Whale-Fishery.* Edinburgh: A. Constable, 1820, vol. 1, p. 472.

Slijper, E. J. *Whales.* London: Hutchinson, 1962. Abridged paperback, Ann Arbor: University of Michigan Press, 1976.
A rich mine of information on the anatomy, physiology, and behavior of cetaceans.

Small, George L. *The Blue Whale.* New York: Columbia University Press, 1971.
Detailed account of the decline of a species under the "protection" of the International Whaling Commission; a National Book Award winner.

Steller, Georg Wilhelm. De Bestiis Marinis [Beasts of the Sea], *Novi Commentarii Academiae Scientarum Imperialis.* vol. 2 [for 1749], 1751, pp. 289–398.

Stephen, David, ed. *Dolphins, Seals and Other Sea Mammals.* New York: Putnam, 1973.
Essentially a collection of color photographs.

Truitt, Deborah. *Dolphins and Porpoises: A Comprehensive Annotated Bibliography of the Smaller Cetacea.* Detroit: Gale Research Co., 1974. Paperback.

Vietmeyer, Noel. "The Endangered but Useful Manatee," *Smithsonian,* vol. 5, no. 9 (December 1974): 60–65.
Describes recent efforts to use manatees in controlling aquatic weeds.

Walker, Theodore J. *Whale Primer, with Special Attention to the Gray Whale.* San Diego, Calif.: Cabrillo

Bibliography

Historical Association, 1975 (rev. ed.). Paperback. Designed mainly for whale watchers at Cabrillo National Monument.

Waters, John F. *Some Mammals Live in the Sea.* New York: Dodd, Mead, 1972.
Written to interest young readers in sea otters, seals, sirenians, and cetaceans.

Wild, Paul W., and Ames, Jack A. *A Report on the Sea Otter,* Enhydra lutris *L., in California.* California Department of Fish and Game, Marine Resources Technical Report no. 20 (1974).
A wildlife management research report.

Wood, Forrest G. *Marine Mammals and Man: The Navy's Porpoises and Sea Lions.* Washington and New York: Robert B. Luce, 1973.
National funding by the military for research on marine mammals is over $1 million a year. This book describes behavioral studies by Navy biologists, especially of seals and porpoises.

INDEX

Living species are indexed by their common names; extinct species by their scientific names. Page numbers in italic type refer to illustrations.

Index

Index

Index

Index